From Little Acorns Grow

A History of
West Bromwich Building Society

From Little Acorns Grow

A History of
West Bromwich Building Society

Professor Carl Chinn

BREWIN BOOKS

First published in 1999 by
Brewin Books, Studley, Warwickshire B80 7LG

New expanded edition July 2006

www.brewinbooks.com

British Library Cataloguing in Publication Data
A catalogue record for this book is available from
The British Library

ISBN: 1 85858 297 0

Typeset in Plantin and made and printed
in Great Britain by Warwick Printing Company Limited

Contents

Acknowledgements

No author can write a book without the help of others. I am no exception and I would like to thank the following people for their help in the writing of the first edition of From Little Acorns, which was published in 1999: Frank Dilkes, former Chairman and Managing Director, for his backing; to present members of the Society, Gordon Hollick for his research work, Steve Brown for his assistance, and Vikki Dukes for her administrative help. I also appreciated the kindness and help provided by the various librarians in Sandwell Department of Education and Community Services, notably Thelma Prentice of Thimblemill Library, Helen Knight, Maureen Waldron, Sam Goode, Claire Harrington and Dawn Winter of Smethwick Library.

It was an enormous pleasure to be asked to update the history of the West Bromwich Building Society to take in the years since the publication of the first edition in 1999. It is often a more difficult task to write contemporary history simply because the author is much closer to the subject and also because there tends to be more material available. That task in writing the new Chapters 6, 7 and 8 has been made easier by the vital support of Jim King, Communications Manager at the Society. Jim provided me with the information that I needed, let me bounce off him early drafts and, in particular, made an essential contribution to Chapter 8. I should also like to thank David Johnston, General Manager (Marketing) at the Society for his input. David made a positive impact on the first edition of this book and he has been a source of guidance throughout the writing of the new chapters. Finally I express my gratitude to Denise McKenzie, Personal Assistant at the Society, for kindly writing up the original chapters 6 and 7 so that I might work on them more easily.

Professor Carl Chinn

July 2006

*The Society's
Principal Office,
374 High Street
(1978).*

Foreword

by Dr Brian Woods-Scawen, Chairman
of West Bromwich Building Society

As Chairman of an organisation that has been in existence for over 150 years, it is a privilege to look back with pride at the imagination, effort and commitment of all those who have helped make the West Bromwich Building Society the successful business it is today.

The Society has, since its formation, held fast to four principles which guide our strategy. They are:

- A commitment to financial success and security for the benefit of our members
- Outstanding service
- A great place for our people to work, learn and develop their careers
- Deep roots in the communities we serve

Not surprisingly, a heritage of over 150 years uncovers episodes of real difficulty, moments of genuine drama, even times when the very survival of the Society has been in doubt. What also emerges, however, is the vision, determination and courage of countless people, who have worked selflessly to ensure that the Society has not simply survived but has succeeded to the point where today we stand proud as one of the UK's top performing building societies.

We are delighted to have the services of the renowned historian, Professor Carl Chinn, who has written this fascinating account of the Society's history. A man with an unrivalled knowledge of the Society's heartlands and great affection for the local area, Professor Chinn is the ideal figure to compile this story.

With its many illustrations and photographs charting the remarkable story of the region's leading building society, the historical journey outlined in *From Little Acorns* reveals many landmarks. Throughout, we can detect those distinctive characteristics of the Society where obstacles are treated as opportunities and challenges become the springboard to innovation and progress.

Many of our members will have read the first edition of this book, which was initially written to celebrate the Society's 150th anniversary in 1999. Writing at the time, Ray Dickinson, the then Chairman of the West Bromwich, spoke of the Society's growth with assets of over £2 billion. In the relatively short time since then, the Society has continued its remarkable rise, more than trebling its assets to over £7 billion. Across every dimension of our operations – lending, savings, profits – we can announce a story of success with record-breaking results year upon year.

Above all, the benefits in better mortgage and savings rates paid to our members as owners of the Society have also reached record levels at more than £30 million in the last financial year. This principle of a business owned by its members lies at the heart of everything we do at the Society. Amidst all our success, the West Bromwich Building Society has never lost sight of that spirit of ownership by its members, which so inspired the Society's founding fathers back in 1849.

Throughout this book you will find evidence of how the Society has always aimed to help ordinary people to better themselves, enabling members to share in our success, and always treating them fairly, honestly and with the utmost integrity. These are fundamental principles and will continue to be the hallmarks of the Society as we move into the future.

From Little Acorns also contains numerous examples of how the Society has reached out to the communities we serve, helping community groups and charitable causes who have turned to the Society for assistance and support. Our branch network extends across the West and East Midlands and spreads into Shropshire and Wales. Wherever we are situated, the Society sees itself as contributing to the heartbeat of local communities. Even as advances in technology have enabled the West Bromwich to become a national name the belief in being rooted in the lives of local communities will remain a foundation of our business.

There is one theme that occurs consistently throughout the whole of *From Little Acorns*. It is that strong sense of commitment to people – our members, our staff and the wider community – which will be our guide as the West Bromwich Building Society continues to grow, thrive and share its success in the future.

Dr Brian Woods-Scawen

Chairman - July 2006

Chapter 1:

For the Benefit of the Working Class, 1775-1859

The Building Society Movement

They were bonded by a firm resolve, that group of twenty men who gathered in the Paradise Street Methodist School Rooms, West Bromwich on 23 April 1849. Their will had to be strong for them to form a permanent building society in the hard days in which they lived. England was in a turbulent state, driven by fierce antagonisms. Employers were ranged against trades unionists, the rich were set against the poor, and the government with all its legal and military powers was held fast against the Chartists – the widespread working-class movement which was striving for democracy. Such fierce tensions were worsened by the woeful state of trade and a dreadful cholera epidemic which killed thousands.

Balance Sheet of West Bromwich Permanent Building Society, 31 May 1851.

BALANCE SHEET
of
THE WEST-BROMWICH PERMANENT BUILDING SOCIETY,

DR.   From April 23rd, 1849, to April 21st, 1851,   CR.

	£ s. d.		£ s. d.
To Cash received for Contributions . . .	422 3 0	By Shares advanced	300 0 0
„ Interest	8 7 6	„ Withdrawn	6 18 9
„ Premiums, extra, ...	7 10 0	**PRELIMINARY EXPENSES IN ESTABLISHING THE SOCIETY, VIZ.**	
„ Tea Party	2 2 0	Books, Stationery, Printing, Advertizing, Postage,	
„ Transfers	2 0	and Enroling Rules . . . , 11 17 10	
„ Fines	5 0	**CURRENT INCIDENTAL EXPENCES, VIZ.**	
ARREARS.		Stationery, &c. 1 2 8	
Contributions 38 14 0	38 14 0		27 13 0
		Rent of Room, Cleaning, and Gas . . . 1 14 0	
		Secretary, on account of Two Years' Salary . . 8 0 0	
		Tea Party in School Room 4 18 6	
		ARREARS.	
		Contributions 38 14 0	
		Balance 105 17 9 144 11 9	
	£479 3 6		£479 3 6

PROFIT OF THE SOCIETY.

Premium on Sale of Two Shares and a half . . . 67 10 0			
Interest 8 7 6		Audited and found correct,	
Transfers 2 0		SAMUEL CASHMORE,	
Fines 5 0		REUBEN FARLEY.	
76 4 6		This 31st day of May, 1851.	
Total expenses of the Society 27 13 0			
£48 11 6			

PRINTED AT THE OFFICE OF THOMAS SMITH, Great-Bridge, West-Bromwich.

Hunger and hardship stalked the land but like others across the country the band of permanent building society pioneers in the Black Country were determined not only to better their own lives but also to improve the conditions of the working class in general. Each wanted to be his own landlord, having the security of living in a home upon which no-one else had a right. Each knew that this desire could be achieved only by joining his savings with those of other like-minded folk for their mutual benefit. In this way the funds could be invested, interest accrued on the capital and monies loaned to members. And each wanted the vote. In a society where class prejudice was rampant, the franchise was restricted to property owners. In these circumstances, the purchase of a house could gain a working man the right to elect a Member of Parliament.

These West Bromwich men were not alone in having the idea of forming a building society. The first in the world had been founded in or before 1775 at the 'Golden Cross' inn at 60, Snow Hill, Birmingham. The 'victualler' at the premises was Richard Ketley, after whom this building society was named. Publicans like himself were often keen to gain trade by attracting meetings and organisations, and licensed houses did figure strongly in the emergence of many bodies aimed at the social welfare of the working class. In particular they were the focal point of friendly societies. Like the Manchester Order of Oddfellows, the Ancient Order of Foresters and others, they charged subscriptions out of which members received benefit in sickness and death.

Plaque commemorating the establishment of the first building society in the world in Snow Hill, Birmingham in 1775.

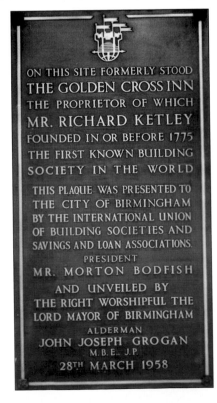

Notice of The Annual Tea Meeting of the West Bromwich Permanent Building Society, 7 June 1852.

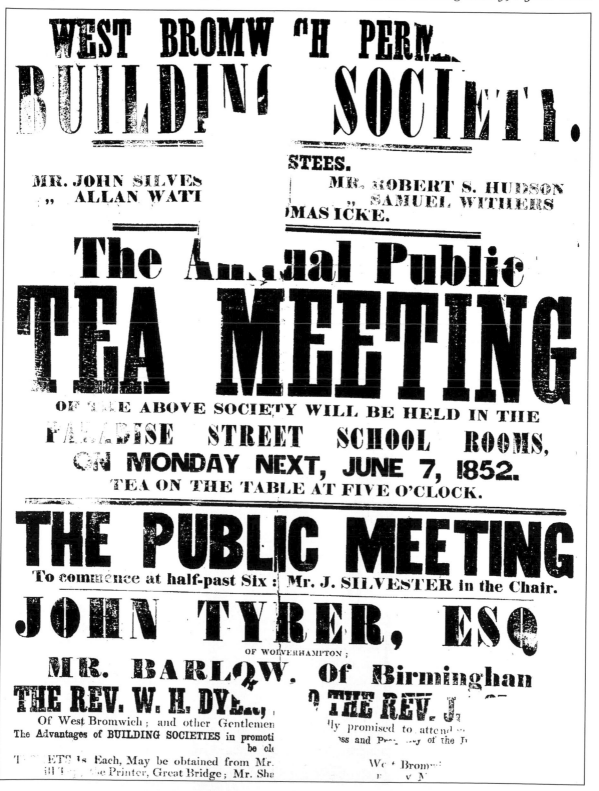

WEST BROMW "H PERM.
BUILDIN SOCIETI.

.....STEES.

MR. JOHN SILVES.....   MR. ROBERT S. HUDSON
    " ALLAN WATI   " SAMUEL WITHERS
    ...MAS ICKE.

The Annual Public
TEA MEETING

OF THE ABOVE SOCIETY WILL BE HELD IN THE

PARADISE STREET SCHOOL ROOMS,
ON MONDAY NEXT, JUNE 7, 1852.

TEA ON THE TABLE AT FIVE O'CLOCK.

THE PUBLIC MEETING

To commence at half-past Six : Mr. J. SILVESTER in the Chair.

JOHN TYRER, ESQ

OF WOLVERHAMPTON ;

MR. BARLOW. Of Birmingham
THE REV. W. H. DYE..,   ? THE REV. J.

Of West Bromwich ; and other Gentlemen
The Advantages of BUILDING SOCIETIES in promoti.....
    be cl.....

...ly promised to attend .....
...ss and Pr.. ..y of the I.....

T....ETS 1s Each, May be obtained from Mr.
.....ill T... ..e Printer, Great Bridge ; Mr. Sha.....

We.. Brom....
.....r .. v N.....

Founded by those who were intent upon helping themselves through combining with others, friendly societies had much in common with the building
societies which followed the example of Ketley's. One of the first to operate on
a large scale was also started in Birmingham in 1781. Its purpose was to erect
houses on the lands of William Jennings in Deritend and its proposed rules were
eight-fold. First, the subscribers had to meet monthly at the 'Fountain' public
house in Cheapside where they would pay the treasurer half a guinea on every
share they took so as to raise a building fund. Second, the subscribers would
elect annually a committee of seven proprietors to run the business of the society.
Third, each subscriber for three shares would have one or more houses built to
the value of 200 guineas. This sum dropped to £140 for those who had two
shares, whilst those with one share would have built a single house worth £70.
Fourth, the rents and profits of such dwellings would be added to the general
fund or stock. Fifth, the committee had the power to contract for the leasing of
the lands intended to be built upon in such proportions as they thought proper.
Terms on these deals would not be less than 110 years and there would be a
ground rent not more than three ha'pence a square yard. Sixth, the society's
rules would be decided by a majority of the subscribers. Seventh, the building
land itself would be split into lots and balloted for by the subscribers. Separate
leases would be made and executed, and they were to stay in the hands of the
society until the proposed buildings were completed. Eighth and last, the first
payment of 10s 6d (52½ pence) was 'to be made this day, the 3rd of December,
1781, when Particulars at large of the peculiar advantages of this Scheme will be
laid before the Meeting'.[1]

By this date there were four building societies in Birmingham and one in
Dudley. Four years later, the Hill House Bank Building Club was set up in
Leeds and by the end of the first decade of the nineteenth century there were
similar societies elsewhere in the north of England, London and Scotland. All
of them were of the terminating type. According to S. J. Price, most set their
shares at £60 or £120. The respective dues of 5s and 10s a month were based
on an assumption that when invested monthly at 5% compound interest the
contributions would grow to the share price after fourteen years.[2] When the
amount of one share was raised it was allocated to a member either through a
ballot or by an auction. This procedure continued until each subscriber had his
house and the society was wound up. To ensure that dues continued to be paid
until then, societies empowered themselves to levy fines on those in arrears and
took other actions. In 1795, in his *History of Birmingham*, William Hutton explained
that 'as a house is a weighty concern, every member is obliged to produce two
bondsmen for the performance of the covenants'.[3]

Hutton added that the building clubs of the town were headed by bricklayers,
and certainly in 1781 Northwood's Building Society had a brickmaker as an
articled servant.[4] Obviously, building trade craftsmen gained work from their
involvement in building societies, but not all such clubs operated in this way. The
Amicable Society of Birmingham (1781) contracted out the construction of its

dwellings, whilst the Rowley Regis Society (1792) authorised its management committee to 'employ men to sink wells or do other work they think shall be proper to buy timber or other materials they shall think proper for the use of building, and to agree with a mason upon the best terms they are able'.[5] At the same time, it is obvious that certain building societies allowed members to construct more than one house, indicating that some properties would be rented out. Still, in theory all societies were mutual in the full meaning of the word. Each person had an equal interest, contributing the same amount to the funds and sharing equally when the society terminated.

As for the type of houses that were built, a house valued at £60 probably would have been a back-to-back – as were those erected by the Crackenthorpe Gardens Building Club in Leeds (1787).[6] Unlike these one-up and one-down structures which had a similar dwelling at their rear, it is most likely that a house worth £120 would have been a two-up and two-down in a terrace unattached to another. More expensive houses could be erected, such as those in Woodcock Street, Birmingham. Here each dwelling in a terrace of fifty three boasted three storeys, elegant doors fronting on to the street, and sash windows with an attractive Georgian look.[7] Presumably such structures were intended for those who lived on the hinterland between the middle and working classes – the likes of shopkeepers, smallscale manufacturers and highly-paid artisans who had served their time in one of the older hand crafts like shoemaking and tailoring.

By the early nineteenth century, building societies were becoming less involved in the actual construction of dwellings and were adopting the practice of the Greenwich Union Society. This was founded in 1809 and its rules allowed a member to receive an advance if he had built a house before his turn. This shift towards making loans for existing property led to another development. Although the principal was accounted for by monthly subscriptions, interest was charged on such advances and the property was mortgaged to the society until the loans were cleared.[8] Other societies charged rent or increased the monthly subscriptions to recuperate their advances and make a profit. Many clubs also began to borrow money from outsiders or more prosperous members so that loans could be made more speedily, whilst increasingly they drew in the savings of small investors – upon which they paid interest.

Because their legal position was ill-defined, some building societies registered under the Friendly Societies Act of 1793, but the first formal recognition of some of their rights came in 1812. This resulted from the test case of 'Pratt versus Hutchinson' when the court ruled that the treasurer of the Greenwich Union Building Society could enforce the payment of arrears by a member. Still it was not until 1836 that the Regulation of Benefit Building Societies Act formally recognised such bodies. This legislation simplified the transfer of property, appointed a barrister to certify the rules of societies and to offer them advice, and exempted them from stamp duty on the movement of shares. The aim was 'to afford encouragement and protection' to building societies, recognising that they were set up by the 'industrious classes, for the purpose of

All Saint's Church, West Bromwich,
about 1900. From the Middle Ages
this was the parish church of West
Bromwich. It was then the main
focal point of the district until the
emergence of the High Street
neighbourhood in the early 1800s.
(with the permission of Sandwell
Community History and Archives Service)

raising by small periodical subscriptions a fund to assist the members thereof in obtaining a small freehold or leasehold property'. There was an ulterior motive to this official support. It was hoped that small depositors would invest in building societies instead of in savings banks. In these, the rate of interest was guaranteed by the government and this backing had led to losses by the Exchequer.[9]

The 1836 Act boosted the number of building societies, but their real growth began after 1845 when James Henry James published a pamphlet on *Benefit Building Societies*. The author was an actuary, an expert in statistics who calculated insurance risks and premiums. He was opposed to terminating societies for two main reasons: after they had started they were difficult to join – given that a new member would have to pay the amount of subscriptions collected already; and they charged borrowers too much. As an improvement, James put forward the principle of permanent societies. These would not dissolve, they would allow people to take shares at any time without having to catch up with the payments of earlier members, and they would set a fixed period for the payment of loans. Consequently it would be easier to work out how much any borrower would have to pay at any time to repay an advance. It was for these reasons that James gave his support to the 1845 constitution of the Metropolitan Equitable Investment Association which offered advances for terms varying from three to fifteen years.[10]

This seems to have been the first permanent building society, and was followed the next year by the National Equitable Building Society, the Wakefield Building Society and the Birmingham No. 4 Building Society. Their principles were explained by G.J. Johnson in 1865:

> it is only *membership* of the individuals composing it which terminates. When any particular member's payments, together with his share of profit during his period of membership, amounts to £120, or whatever may be the prescribed amount of the share, he must be paid out if he is an investor; if he is a borrower he must continue to pay until not only his £120 but also the premium he agreed to pay for the advance of that sum is made up. The advantages of this permanent plan are numerous; e.g. the members can join at any time without paying any arrears, and the proportion between borrowers and investors is steadier than in terminating societies.[11]

Based on these two groups, investors and borrowers, permanent societies gained popularity. Their growth was stimulated by the publication of Arthur Scratchley's *Treatise on Benefit Building Societies*. As another actuary and founder of the London and Metropolitan Counties Society (1848) he was intimately associated with the building society movement. According to S.J. Price, the book published in 1849 'must have been very influential in spreading the permanent principle'.[12] It was easier to read than the work by James and importantly for the effective running of a building society it provided tables for the calculation of interest and repayments.

Dartmouth Square and High Street, West Bromwich about 1910. Looking towards New Street, on the left is the fountain (now in Dartmouth Park) and in the foreground is an electric tram. (with the permission of Sandwell Community History and Archives Service)

The idea of permanent building societies was boosted further by the emergence of freehold land societies. Following the Great Reform Act of 1832, the economic advantages of house ownership were bolstered by political benefits. This had decreed that to gain the franchise in a borough such as Birmingham a man had to be renting property valued at £10 for local rates, whilst in the counties like Staffordshire he had to be a 40 shilling (£2) freeholder. This meant that he owned property worth £40 based on an annual 5% return. At a time when agricultural labourers were earning as little as 7 shillings (35 pence) a week, such thresholds were out of the reach of the great majority of the working class. But there was some hope for skilled and better paid working men. The borough qualification was too far out of their reach, but even a back-to-back worth £60 could confer the right to vote if it was located in the shires.

Vendors were alert to the attractiveness of such properties, which became even more desirable after the emergence of Chartism in 1838.[13] This mass movement sought to end privilege by the extension of the franchise to all adult men. Petitions were raised and presented to Parliament to reform itself, but no progress was made given the undemocratic nature of both the House of Commons and the House of Lords. Radical working men realised that more of their supporters needed to be returned as MPs if change were to occur. As a result, some activists bonded together in small groups to purchase land and property in the shires.

A series of legal cases determined that if such purchases were in good faith they did pass on the franchise. But there remained a major problem which prevented large-scale enfranchisement. The 1836 Act forbade the ownership of land by building societies. Without their resources it seemed as if there could be no widespread land acquisitions which could give the vote to the many instead of the few. A way round this problem was devised by James Taylor, a descendant of the Brummagem button king who had been instrumental in founding Lloyd's Bank in Dale End, Birmingham in 1765. A Non-Conformist in religion and democrat in politics, Taylor had been motivated by the defeat of the pro-reform Liberal candidate in the North Warwickshire election of August 1847. Going to the hustings:

> I saw hundreds of hard-working men, standing and looking on, grinning and yawning over the poles which separated them from the voters – they had dirty hands and brown faces. I thought they ought to have the votes, and I determined that they should have votes if I could help them to obtain them.[14]

Within a month Taylor and his friends had begun the Birmingham Freehold Land Society. Its objectives were 'to elevate the social – promote the moral – exalt the political – and improve the pecuniary condition of the unenfranchised and labouring classes'. The scheme itself worked by finding a group of interested people to buy an estate and sell it on in plots of £2. These could be bought by the members of a building society by way of advances. In the case of the Birmingham

Freehold Land Society, its loans were made to members of the Birmingham and Midland Counties' Benefit Building Society. Glorying in slogans such as 'Possess the Land', 'County Votes for Working Men' and 'Freeholds for the People', the land society charged an entrance fee of 1 shilling with a payment of 3 shillings per fortnight and 6 pence per share each quarter.[15] At such rates it would have taken a member eight years to buy a £30 share, and so ballots of members were held to speed up matters.

The first plot of land was bought in January 1848 at Handsworth, then a district in Staffordshire, and four months later members marched in a grand and triumphant procession to take possession of the site. Within months, other freehold land societies had sprung up at Dudley and Wolverhampton in the Black Country. Once again where the West Midlands led the rest of the country followed, and by the summer of 1849 like-minded societies had been set up in Worcester, Derby, Sheffield, Newcastle-upon-Tyne and elsewhere. One of the most important was London's National Freehold Land Society, which became the National Building Society, the forerunner of the Abbey National Building Society in 1894. By this date the Birmingham Freehold Land Society was effectively part of the Birmingham Incorporated Building Society.

The Emergence of the Town of West Bromwich

All building societies were associated with men who were prudent, pragmatic, aspiring and motivated. And all were products of a society which was expanding, industrialising, urbanising and youthful. West Bromwich itself typified these features which were transforming England into the wealthiest and most powerful nation in the world. Called by F.W. Hackwood 'the Chicago of Modern England', it had developed as rapidly as a recently-settled American city.[16] From its mention in the Domesday Book of 1086 as the manor of 'Bromwich', the area had remained agricultural and sparsely populated until the arrival of nail makers like the Turtons in the late seventeenth century. Even then there was no effective centre to West Bromwich. Instead its folk were scattered about the hamlets at Hall Green, Bird's End, Gold's Green, Hill Top, Lyndon, Mayer's Green, Virgin's End, Overend, Cutler's or Lambert's End (now Dartmouth Street), and Old or Moore's End. These small settlements partly surrounded the great common and wastes of West Bromwich on which local people grazed their animals. Almost 400 acres of land, it was crossed by the main road from Birmingham and upon it was only one house.[17]

In August 1776, Arthur Young went from Birmingham to West Bromwich and wrote that for five or six miles the road was 'one continued village of nailers'.[18] Despite this comment, most of West Bromwich was still rural – but its rapid and overwhelming change was heralded four years later when the Turtons' water mill on the Oldbury Road was taken over by Izon and Whitehurst of Birmingham, manufacturers of hinges and small iron goods. The partners had been attracted to their new position by a number of factors: a site which was larger than their existing cramped premises; a power supply from water – although a second-hand Boulton and Watt steam engine was soon bought; the closeness of the premises to the Birmingham Canal, which had been opened in 1772 to allow the fast and cheap transport of coal from Wednesbury to Birmingham; and the emergence of South Staffordshire as a major iron-producing region.[19]

Good communications and a supply of raw materials also appealed to Archibald Kenrick. Originally a Brummagem buckle maker, when his trade declined, Kenrick shifted into the making of cast ironmongery. In 1791 he fastened upon a site for production in Spon Lane, West Bromwich. Like Izon's factory it was on the Birmingham Canal, whilst it also benefited from its proximity to the main road which connected Birmingham via West Bromwich to Shrewsbury and Holyhead in North Wales. Fourteen years later, Kenricks added the manufacture of hollow ware to their operations.[20] At the other end of West Bromwich, another industrial development was initiated by Luke and Jesse Siddons who started the Hill Top Foundry in 1799. Just under fifty years later, two of their descendants began another renowned cast iron hollow-ware business – J. and J. Siddons Ltd which specialised in the production of cooking utensils.[21]

The Wesley Chapel in High Street, West Bromwich, about 1893.

Positioned on the south-eastern edge of a Black Country which was becoming one of the most important industrial regions internationally, West Bromwich was also close to a Birmingham which was rushing to become one of the greatest manufacturing towns in the world. This favourable location ensured that other industrialists would soon switch their focus to a place which still had a population of only about 4,000 at the end of the eighteenth century. A major impetus to growth came in 1802 when the open common was divided, allotted and enclosed. To compensate them for the loss of grazing rights all freeholders of the parish gained some of the enclosed ground, although the largest landlords gained the most – such as the Earl of Dartmouth of Sandwell Hall. Initially most of the owners cultivated their new property but by 1829 the old heath where rabbits had burrowed was 'not now to be recognised; the habitations of men and establishments of artisans have sprung up with surprising rapidity; and from a place insignificant in its origin, West Bromwich has become important in its trade and manufactures, with a population enterprising and respectable'.[22]

Focused on its High Street, a new town had emerged. Swiftly it eclipsed the older hamlets in size and importance. This change was recognised officially in 1828 when the West Bromwich Post Office was moved from Hill Top to 382, High Street. The following year on the same thoroughfare Christ Church was consecrated to provide a place of worship that was easier to reach for the bulk of the population than was the Old Church of All Saints. It was followed in 1835 by the opening of the Wesley Chapel just up from New Street. Later known as St. George's Hall, this replaced the chapel in Paradise Street. By now the 'Dartmouth Hotel' on the corner of Spon Lane and High Street had also become the main meeting place for the wealthy of the town.

The growth of the High Street locality led to an extraordinary rise in population. In the decade from 1821 it shot up by 5,822 to reach 15,377. Yet for all the building of new houses and the cutting of new streets, the place 'retained much of its rural condition'.[23] There was a toll gate near the end of Dartmouth Street, a wake was held annually on the corner of Paradise Street across from Barrow Street, and Heath Terrace still overlooked the remnants of the common. This rural feel soon disappeared from much of West Bromwich. Attracted by extensive ironworks and collieries like that in Pitt Street, migrants poured into the town from elsewhere in Staffordshire as well as from Shropshire, Warwickshire and Worcestershire. By 1851, immigration and a nationally-high birth rate had swelled the population of the town to almost 35,000.

As West Bromwich expanded so too did the reputation of its wares. The town was well known for its coal, chains, cables, stoves, grates, coffee-mills and general ironmongery – and if it was true that there were 'few civilised countries which do not import English hollow-ware' then much of it came from Izons, Kenricks and Siddons. Two other manufacturers were marked out for their fame: firstly, spring makers such as George Salter and Co., dating back locally to 1790, and A.A. James of Lombard Street; and secondly, producers of sad irons (solid

The meat mincer finishing shop at Izons and Co. of West Bromwich.

flat-irons) and box irons. Along with Kenricks, this trade was carried on by William Bullock and Co. of Spon Lane, Enoch Siddaway and Sons of George Street and William Cross and Son of Bond Street. Later, they were joined by the Siddons. Interestingly the family had once been publicans of the 'Box Iron' in Hill Top.[25] In addition to these concerns were others such as Robinson Brothers, founded in 1869 as a tar and ammonia distilling business in Ryders Green. Now suppliers of chemical intermediates, Robinsons is one of the largest manufacturing employers in West Bromwich.[26]

Praised by the American observer Elihu Burritt as 'a place of much vigour and growth', West Bromwich was a largely working-class town.[27] And it was in the heroic age of working-class self-advancement that twenty local men met with the firm intent of making a mark. Resolved to start the West Bromwich Building Society, they chose a significant day for their action – for 23 April was not only St. George's Day but also it was Shakespeare's Birthday. Linking themselves so specifically with England's national day and its most revered writer, the founders of the West Bromwich Building Society were emphasising their patriotism and their rights as freeborn Englishmen. These pioneers were as careful in deciding upon their

Staff and workpeople of Robinson Brothers Limited, about 1930.

number, as twenty was the rule for terminating societies. Importantly, however, the West Bromwich men were determined that their society should be permanent in its nature. There is no doubt that they were innovators, for the West Bromwich Building Society was one of the earliest such bodies. Other forerunners included the Woolwich Equitable, started in 1847 by members who had broken away from a terminating society; the Leeds Permanent Building Society, which began in November 1848 as a successor to a previous terminating society and which soon proclaimed itself the largest building society in the world; and the Planet Building Society, also started in 1848 by members of Wesley's Chapel, City Road, London.

The Origins and Aims of the West Bromwich Building Society

Significantly, the driving spirits of the West Bromwich Building Society first met in the day schools which once had been the Paradise Street Methodist Chapel. John Wesley himself, the charismatic preacher who initiated the sect, had preached there when it was known as the 'Room'.[28] Their choice of venue is suggestive. Methodism was strong in the Black Country and here as elsewhere it was associated with working-class men and women who prized respectability, hard work, thrift and independence. They were also imbued with an egalitarian spirit. Compared with the Church of England from which it had broken Methodism was 'essentially a layman's religion'.[29] Members of congregations were given the opportunities to become involved in the leadership and running of their chapels, whilst they were provided with the means for self-education. These features meant that Methodists became noticeable as leaders in Chartism, trade unionism and the co-operative movement – which itself expanded after the opening of a retail shop in Rochdale in 1844.

The trailblazers of the West Bromwich Permanent Building Society had much in common with their fellows in other working-class movements. Out of the twenty of them, there is certain information about the occupations of thirteen. Four were retailers: both Joseph Hughes and James P. Sharp were shop-keepers and dealers in groceries and sundries; Charles Cottrell was a butcher; and George Coleman was a corn flour dealer. Throughout England, many such men were intimately tied to the working class through their background, trade and sympathies. Such considerations applied to the three other men in business – the boat builder, James Steventon; the blacksmith, William Upton; and the spring balance maker, Enoch Silvester.

The rest of the founders were workers: both W.H. Lewis and Henry Millward were boot and shoe makers; John Harley was a carpenter and joiner; William Dangerfield was an engineer; Lot Shakespeare – aptly named considering that the first meeting took place on the birthday of William Shakespeare – was a coal miner; and Samuel Withers was a glass cutter. Of this last group, five were definitely in skilled occupations. There was one possible exception, Shakespeare. The definition of a coal miner included a wide range of distinct jobs, some of which were unskilled, but if Shakespeare was a hewer who dug the coal at the face then he would have been regarded as one of the elite amongst coal miners. It is interesting that two men were cobblers. As members of an older hand-craft they would have been classed as artisans. In general such men were noted for their radical views, whilst shoemakers in particular were in the forefront of working-class political activity. Of the remaining three men, engineers and carpenters were also perceived as belonging to the aristocracy of labour whilst Samuel Withers the glass cutter was another who definitely would have been seen as skilled.[30]

Crucially, the Withers family was intimately bonded with the origins and growth of Methodism in West Bromwich. Samuel's aunt, Rebecca Alcock, had heard John Wesley preach locally in the late eighteenth century, whilst his father was described as one of the pioneers of the movement in the district. Samuel Withers the elder was a devoted worker to the cause, 'walking Sunday after Sunday to the little wayside Chapel on the right side of the road leading to Barr'.[31] This was close to the site of the Newton Road home of Francis Asbury, the Great Barr preacher who was responsible for the spread of Methodism in the United States of America.[32] One of his older sons, Thomas, was as deeply committed to the cause of Methodism. He had been educated at the Paradise Street Chapel Sunday School when 'the method of writing was to place before the pupil a pan or trough of sand, shaken level, the words being formed by the forefinger of the scholar'. In later life he became the first superintendent of Park Village Sunday School which met in an upstairs room until a school chapel was built in Roebuck Street.[33]

Francis Asbury, the Great Barr man who was crucial in spreading the beliefs of Methodism across the United States of America.

If religious beliefs may have had an effect on the founders of West Bromwich Permanent Building Society, then political convictions certainly had an influence. No records survive of either the inaugural meeting or the first annual report, but in the second annual report of 31 May 1851 the committee earnestly appealed 'to the Working Classes to avail themselves of the advantages of this society, and thereby become their own landlords'.[34] The class-based origins of the West Bromwich were emphasised five years later when it was recommended 'to *Working Men* as an institution devised for their benefit, and . . . suited to their wants'.[35] Importantly the bonds between class, house ownership and reform were also made plain. In 1852 it was stressed that through joining the Society a working man 'may eventually become his own landlord, and enjoy the privilege of exercising the franchise'.[36]

Third Annual Report of West Bromwich Permanent Building Society, 1852.

THIRD ANNUAL REPORT
OF THE
WEST BROMWICH PERMANENT BUILDING SOCIETY.

THE Committee, in presenting their Third Annual Report, congratulate the Members on the progress of the Society during the past year, the number of members having increased from 62 to 104, who are the Proprietors of 119 shares of £20 each, equivalent to a prospective accumulated capital of £14,280. The success and stability of the Society is therefore established in a complete and satisfactory manner.

Shares have been sold during the year amounting to the sum of £480, which has been advanced on good Freehold Securities, situate at High Street, in the Parish of West Bromwich, and at Toll End, in the Parish of Tipton.

The transactions of the year give a profit of TWENTY-FIVE PER CENT., which has been placed to the credit of each individual Member's account.

The attention of the Public is requested to the facilities this Society presents for the safe deposit of money in small or large sums, either as temporary or permanent investments; and while the Society is equal in security to Savings' Banks, it enjoys the important advantage of yielding a larger interest.

Every working man will do well to reflect that by contributing to this Society half-a-crown per week, he may eventually become his own landlord, and enjoy the privilege of exercising the franchise.

No entrance money required. The next three nights of meeting are May 31st, June 14th and 28th, at the Paradise Street School Rooms, West Bromwich, from seven till nine o'clock.

BALANCE SHEET OF
The West Bromwich Permanent Building Society,
FOR THE YEAR ENDING APRIL 19, 1852.

	£	s.	d.		£	s.	d.
To Balance from last year	105	17	9	By Shares advanced to Members	480	0	0
„ Contributions to Share Fund	505	18	9	„ Ditto withdrawn	78	7	9
„ Interest	33	7	6	„ Insurance	0	17	9
„ Extra Premiums	32	10	0	„ Deposit repaid and Interest	51	1	10
„ Deposit	50	0	0				
„ Fines	2	7	0	CURRENT INCIDENTAL EXPENSES—			
„ Transfer	0	2	0	„ Sundry Accounts £12 17 6			
„ Rules	0	0	6	„ Postage, Stationery, &c. 1 11 7			
ARREARS.				„ One Year's Rent of Room 1 1 0			
„ Contributions £4 0 0				„ Arrears due to Secretary 1 2 0			
„ Insurance 0 17 9—4 17 9				„ Secretary's Salary 9 2 0			
				„ Steward's ditto 1 2 9—26 16			
				ARREARS.			
				„ By Contributions £4 0 0			
				„ Balance in hand 93 17 1—97			
	£735	1	3		£73		

Examined and found correct this 14th day of May, 1852,

REUBEN FARLEY,
WILLIAM S. REEVES, } AUDITORS.

JAMES P. SHARP, SECRETARY

PROFITS OF THE SOCIETY FOR THE YEAR.

To Premiums on Sale of Shares..........£120
„ Interest on Purchased Shares..........33
„ Fines..........2
„ Transfers..........

By Expenses of the Society..........£96 16
„ Interest on Deposit....

These democratic credentials of the West Bromwich were reinforced by its affirmation in 1853 that 'any person whether male or female is eligible to be a member'. This was a radical principle in a period when no woman had the vote and when the law did not recognise that a wife could have her own property.[37] Indeed the first Married Women's Property Act was not passed until 1870. Perhaps because of its adherence to democratic principles, the founders of the West Bromwich faced some opposition – for in 1862 it was claimed that when the Society had been formed 'grave doubts' had been expressed and 'strong prejudice' had existed against its success.[38]

The gaining of the vote through house purchase was intimately associated both with individual betterment and the collective progress of the working class. These powerful connections were made plain in the ninth annual report on 13 April 1857.

And as the paramount object of this Society is the improvement of the condition and the social elevation of the Working Classes, by enabling them to become (upon easy terms) the owners of House Property, your Committee would gladly welcome to their ranks a large accession of members belonging to that class, whose lot in life it is to get their bread by the sweat of their brow. Believing further that this Society has a tendency to encourage and foster habits of prudence and economy, your Committee are desirous of seeing its sphere of influence enlarged.[39]

Swanpool, West Bromwich, 1907 – known locally as Wasson Pool.
(with the permission of Sandwell Community History)

Similar sentiments were recorded in the prospectus of the Coventry Provident Building Society in 1872. This proclaimed itself as presenting 'the most favourable inducements to the working man; it enables him to accumulate his savings at compound interest, and, by small payments to the Society, it will be in the power of the humblest individual to become the owner of the house he inhabits'.[40]

It seems apparent that the Society targeted the skilled and well-paid of the working class. This was the group which was most imbued with notions of collective action and thus was most likely to join organisations that adhered to that ideal – such as co-operatives, friendly societies, trade unions and building societies. The committee recognised the potent appeal of mutuality and in its eighth annual report on 13 May 1857 explained that 'all profits made are justly divided among the members'. This readiness to appreciate the concerns of the prosperous of the working class was highlighted by the committee's appreciation of the fact that even better-off folk could be plunged into poverty through misfortune and so lose their status in the community. Accordingly in its rules the West Bromwich made provisions to meet *'loss of work, loss of health, or removal'*, whilst 'those who borrow money to build or buy houses or to repay mortgages are not liable to have it suddenly called in at a short notice as in private mortgages; the money so had is repaid to the Society by easy instalments'. By such actions the Society sought to adapt itself to the 'wants, means and condition' of the 'industrious working classes'.[41]

Although no entrance fee was charged, weekly dues of 2s 6d (12½p) a week towards the purchase of a full £120 share do corroborate the interpretation that the West Bromwich was set up by and for comfortably-off members of the working class. No membership lists survive, so definitive corroboration cannot be put forward. But there is a suggestive piece of evidence provided by William Kenrick in 1866. He mentioned that within the cast iron hollow-ware and tinned, enamelled and cast ironmongery trades the 'wages of skilled workers average from 25 shillings to 40 shillings'. He added that 'it may be taken as an evidence of provident habits in this class of workmen under favourable circumstances that, of the number employed by one firm, one-fifth are freeholders'. It is highly probable that this firm was that of Kenrick's own family in Spon Lane. Given their factory's location in West Bromwich it is feasible to suppose that a substantial proportion of those freeholders may have been members of the West Bromwich Permanent Building Society.[42]

Compared to the hollow-ware workers, it is most unlikely that nailors were noticeable amongst the early members. Although well-established locally, their prosperity lay well in the past and increasingly they were under pressure from the large and mechanised nail manufacturers of Birmingham. By the mid-nineteenth century, wages for male nailors in the Black Country were depressed, ranging from 7 shillings (35p) to 16 shillings (80p) a week. Women earned half as much as the men and children half as much again.[43] In many families the combined earnings would have been less than the 21 shillings (£1.05p) which was set as the poverty line for a man, woman and a moderate family as late as

1914. On such levels it would have been almost impossible for nailors to have contributed an eighth or more of their weekly income as dues to a building society. The ordeals of the nailors are graphically recounted in the novel *A Capful O' Nails* (1879) by David Christie Murray. The son of a printer cum bookseller,

Balance Sheet and Statement of Accounts of West Bromwich Permanent Building Society, 11 April 1859.

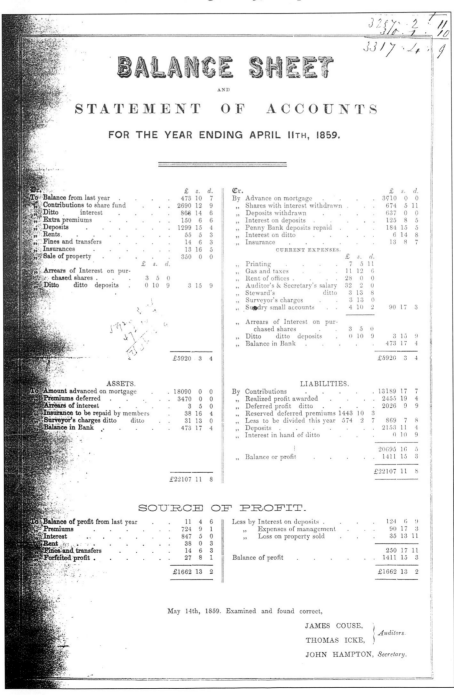

he was born in the High Street of West Bromwich in 1847. After some time in the army he became a journalist and then an author. Although his books never achieved widespread fame, *A Capful O' Nails* is an evocative and intuitive work. There is a memorial tablet to Murray in West Bromwich Central Library.[44]

Nailors were not the only workers enduring hard times in the 1850s. In its second annual report (31 May 1851) the committee of the West Bromwich explained that as the Society 'commenced its existence at a period of commercial embarrassment, little progress was made during the first year'. Subscribers had increased only from thirty to seventy one – although 'this is without any further public announcement having been made than the advertisement of its formation'. None of them was in arrear, but their combined dues totalled just £422 3s 0d. Moreover, despite its avowed intent to help in the purchase of houses the West Bromwich did not appear to have made advances for mortgages in the period between 23 April 1849 and 31 May 1851.[45] In this regard it compared unfavourably with the Burnley Building Society formed in 1850 to 'devise a plan whereby the working classes might be induced to make small savings and thus create habits of thrift and frugality'. After its first year, it had balances due on mortgages of £1,458 and a capital account of £1,980.[46]

The objectives of the West Bromwich were clear: 'to enable its Members to acquire Property by the fruits of their own honest industry and frugality – in other words to build or purchase Dwelling Houses, or some other Freehold, Copyhold, or Leasehold Property from a common Fund, raised by Members' contributions paid fortnightly'.[47] Despite this intent the first advances by the West Bromwich were not indicated until the third annual report on 14 May 1852. Four shares were sold, the returns from which had been advanced on 'good Freehold Securities' in High Street, West Bromwich and Toll End, Tipton. The committee also drew attention to the facilities provided by the Society for 'the safe deposit of money in large or small sums as either temporary or permanent investments; and while the Society is equal to Savings Banks, it enjoys the important advantage of yielding a larger income'.[48]

Two years later the Society had moved from Paradise Street, where it tended to have meetings twice a month, to its first regular office at 402, Lower High Street, close to the bank. It was fitted out and provided with fire proof safes for deeds and books. By now James P. Sharp had been appointed as secretary and the committee felt that the Society was 'making rapid progress'. In reality, with an income of £2,917 2s 2d progress had been slow but steady.[49] It continued to be so despite 'the precarious state of trade' in 1854/55 and the 'commercial panic of unprecedented severity' which sorely affected West Bromwich three years later.[50] Indeed, it was not until the 1860s that the affairs of the Society would prosper sufficiently to justify the assertion that its progress was 'more rapid and unchecked'. And as it advanced, so too did it become obvious that the Society itself was changing in its nature.

Chapter 2:

More Rapid and Unchecked Growth, 1860-1913

The Development of the West Bromwich Building Society

As the 1850s waned, the committee of the West Bromwich acknowledged that 'in the first two or three years of its existence, the amount of business transacted was of a limited character'. Despite this unpromising beginning the founders had not been disheartened, rather they 'were fortified in the belief' that there was a need for a building society locally and that 'with increase of age it would gain strength and influence'. By 1860 it seemed that these hopes had been achieved. It was reported that without any outside help, great strides forward had been made in the previous two years so that 'a position and a reputation inferior to no other similar society in Staffordshire' had been attained. Since the financial report of 1858, 105 new members had been added and only eighteen had withdrawn. This increase almost doubled the membership to 186, whilst the balance sheet was also 'something wonderful'. Total annual receipts from all sources were just above £6,916 – 'a sum unparalleled in the annals of the society' and £1,000 more than the previous year.[1]

This growth was associated with the expansion of building societies generally, so that by 1860 there were over 750 in London and 2,000 elsewhere in England and Wales. That year it was revealed that the West Bromwich had co-operated with 'other kindred Societies' to oppose the proposal by the Chancellor of the Exchequer to end their exemption from stamp duties. All constitutional means in 'their power' were used to support the campaign. Letters were written to the two Parliamentary members for Staffordshire and a deputation was appointed 'to wait upon Mr Gladstone'. It was not needed. The Chancellor withdrew his resolution.[2] This was an interesting and important indication of nationwide contact nine years before both *The Building Societies' Gazette* was started and the Building Societies Protection Association was formed in London by James Higham.

Further gains were made by the West Bromwich in 1861, with receipts rising to a little over £7,207 and 101 new members joining. This improvement was achieved in the face of depressed trade locally and it led the committee to proclaim that the Society was now making 'more rapid and unchecked' progress.[3] In the succeeding years the Society's affairs continued to flourish for two reasons: first, the need for housing locally; and second, a generally favourable economic climate. The town of West Bromwich had not yet reached its limits, and in the four years from 1871 it was believed that the population had grown by 800 annually to reach 51,200. Unfortunately there was 'a lamentable deficiency of house accommodation' even though land was still available for building. These circumstances signified that there was a market for mortgages and that 'there is a great future for the West Bromwich Permanent Building Society'.[4]

The need for houses coincided with the so-called Mid-Victorian Boom. This period can be regarded in too optimistic a light and it is doubtful whether the unskilled, the widowed, the disabled and others of the poor benefited from any betterment in trade. Still it was a time of prosperity for many of those who were skilled and in regular work – the kind of people most likely to be attracted to joining building societies. Their relative affluence and the 'flourishing condition' of the staple trades of the region meant that by 1878 the membership of the West Bromwich had swollen to 2,368, whilst its assets had burgeoned to £163,790 11s 1d. With justifiable satisfaction the committee pointed out that its dividend of 6%, apportioned at 1s 2d in the pound, proved that joining the Society was 'a wise and judicious investment' considering that it was safe, free from risk and of undoubted security.[5]

The Development of Building Societies

That year the assets of the West Bromwich compared favourably with those of the Bingley Building Society which stood at £218,666. Interestingly, two years previously and with assets of just under £50,000 the Yorkshire-based society had lagged significantly behind its Black Country counterpart, which boasted a figure of almost £140,000. Yet if the West Bromwich had been outstripped in a time of affluence its steady approach was more successful during the subsequent and long-term depression. The Bingley was not to exceed its 1878 total for another twenty years, whilst the West Bromwich continued to grow slowly but surely.[6] The next year, the committee of the West Bromwich glowingly declared that over the past thirty years its business had multiplied by 276. Receipts now totalled £55,297, as opposed to £200 in the first year; advances on mortgages had reached £26,721, by contrast to a mere £300 in both 1849 and 1850; and membership was up to 2,415, even though new additions had been small because of 'the long depression'.[7]

By this time all building societies were subject to the requirements of an Act of Parliament passed in 1874. This restricted the liability of members to the arrears due from them or to the amount actually owing under the mortgage; it limited borrowing powers to two-thirds of the amount secured on the mortgage; it decreed that officers having charge of money should give security for the proper discharge of their duties; it allowed a society itself, rather than trustees, to hold mortgage deeds and stand security for loans; it enjoined all new societies to be incorporated under the Act and enabled older societies to do so; and it restricted

Mrs. Selina Horton's statement of account regarding her contributions to the share fund of West Bromwich Permanent Building Society, 30 June 1873. (thanks to Colin Woodward of Bilston, who found this share certificate amongst his father's effects; and Sue K. Johnson of the Bilston Branch Office)

Share No. 2773

West Bromwich Permanent Building Society,

HIGH STREET, JUNE 30th, 1873.

Mr. *S. Horton*

Sir,

I beg to hand you a Statement of your Account as per the Society's Ledger.

	£	s.	d.
By Contributions to Share Fund to April 22nd, 1873.	13	15	
By Realized Profit to April 24, 1872		4	4
„ Deferred „ „ 24, „		2	9
„ Profit added this year being 1s. 2d. in the £ on the Contributions & Realized Profit		16	5
Total	£15	1	6

If you withdraw your Contributions before they, with the Profit, reach the amount for which you entered the Society, the Profit is forfeited, but interest at the rate of four per cent. per annum is allowed.

Yours respectfully,

JOHN HAMPTON,

Secretary.

the investment of surplus funds to mortgages or securities with a government guarantee. This prevented direct investment in land or other property and in companies. Finally, mergers were discouraged by the stipulation that amalgamations and transfers of engagements required the consent of three-quarters of the members involved and that they must hold at least two-thirds of the total value of shares.

Although the 1874 Act provided the legal framework under which building societies operated over the next 100 years, its effectiveness was hindered by the lack of procedures for enforcing many of its provisions. Nor did its overall tenor appeal to most existing societies. The majority were still terminating and the 1874 Act greatly restricted the heavy borrowing they needed in their early years, whilst if they were close to termination there was no reason at all for them to change the way they operated. Similarly, many permanent societies were put off incorporation by the need to change rules and take on new responsibilities. More importantly they were deterred by the loss of exemption from stamp duties and the ending of the role of trustees, men who had been chosen for their assiduity and integrity.

Facing Problems

With the Society's affairs flourishing, the committee of the West Bromwich did not see the need to incorporate. The self-confidence of the Society in its existing status was highlighted in 1881 when it was stated that there were 946 building societies in England and Wales with an average membership of 330 and receipts for 1880/81 of £17,037. By contrast the West Bromwich had 2,551 members and an income of £61,701, making it plain that the Society 'ranks very high' in the movement as a whole.[8] Although prospering in spite of the continuing economic problems nationally and locally, the West Bromwich was faced with two major concerns in the early 1880s: members who were in difficulties because of the economic downturn withdrew large amounts of money; and there was a large deposit of its funds at its bank. This sum earned less money than was possible via mortgages. It was realised that in order to make the income of the Society yield a satisfactory return then it was 'necessary that there should be an increasing number of borrowing Members'. For several years it was reiterated that 'having regard to the present prices of Labour and Building Materials, and of the value of House Property, the present is a favourable time for acquiring that class of Property, either by building or by purchase'. By these means, the members of the West Bromwich could make 'some kind of provision against bad times and old age, and for those dependent upon them by the ties of Nature and of Kindred'.[9]

The Society was not alone in its predicament. Prices, interest rates and property values were falling throughout the country. In this situation building societies were able to draw in more savings by maintaining their mortgage rates. Yet the slump in the property market and the rising amount of surplus funds ensured that 'demand for loans backed by adequate mortgage security was inadequate to absorb the societies' funds'.[10] This often led to competition between societies which tried to outdo one another in making generous advances against poor security. Other initiatives led some into financing commercial enterprises and to acting more as banks. There is no evidence of the West Bromwich adopting

West Bromwich Permanent Benefit Building Society,
'Home Sweet Home' advertisement on cloth, about 1890.

Home, Sweet Home

Even if there is rent to pay it is still a place dear to an Englishman, but how much pleasanter when it is really your own. "No rent to pay." Not subject to seven days' notice to leave, no forfeiting any improvements you may have made. If you pay 5s. or 6s. per week rent for 20 or 30 years it is no nearer your own than it was the first month you entered it, but for 5s. per week you could have from the

West Bromwich Permanent Benefit Building Society

£200 to enable you to buy or build a House, and if you found the money for the land, you would get as good a House as you are now paying 5s. 6d. per week rent for, and with this advantage, the House by every payment is gradually becoming your own. If you wish to pay it off quicker, you can pay 6s. 8d. per week for each £200 borrowed, and at the same rate in proportion for larger or smaller amounts, with this further advantage, that while the Society cannot call in the amount if you keep good the payments agreed to, you can pay in any extra you wish and thereby lessen the interest and hasten the completion of your payments.

If you do not wish to build or buy House Property, but are anxious to make some provision for "a rainy day," you cannot do better than enter the investment branch of the Society, the payments of which is 5s. per fortnight for each share of £120. You can in this department withdraw in 14 days the whole or any part paid in with interest.

Subscription nights every alternate week on Monday and Tuesday.

Office open every Wednesday night, from 6-30 to 8-30, to answer enquiries.

JOHN HAMPTON, Secretary.

these short-termist strategies. It prided itself on 'prudent and judicious management' and doggedly maintained its commitment to investments only on freehold or leasehold houses, 'not upon Land only nor upon Works or Speculative Buildings'. Still there is no doubt that the Society was affected by the harsh economic realities. By 1884 the adverse 'condition of the Coal and Iron Trade, and of the wage-earning classes of West Bromwich and the surrounding district' had led to a decrease in the volume of business for the first time since 1870. This was apparent in both the receipts to the share fund and the amount lent on mortgage. The resultant dividend of 4½% (11d in the £) was also lower than usual but it was asserted that it was still good value when compared to the 2% paid by the Bank of England and the high of 4% given by railway shares and high-class debentures.

Two years later, in 1886, the West Bromwich was forced to a shift in its policies because of the changes 'in the value of Real Estate and in the earning power of money'. It revised 'the Rules and Scales of repayment' and at the same time stressed that the 'Society offers to Borrowers with good Securities, advantages exceeding those which are attainable in any similar Societies in this district'. Every available facility was now offered to borrowing members and it was with confidence that members were urged to bring 'these advantages before their friends, and by these means to extend the operations and usefulness of the West Bromwich Permanent Building Society'. In spite of these changes, the decision was soon taken not to take any further deposits. Lifted temporarily early in 1888, the ban was swiftly reintroduced until 'the £9,000 lying at the Bank on deposit, can be advanced to members upon satisfactory securities at an early date'.[14]

In 1890 this strategy was followed by another whereby charges on advances to borrowers were reduced to 5% per year – 'which it is expected will be an inducement to members to build or to buy House Property'. Furthermore, where business resulted the Society would now pay the surveyor's charges for the valuation of such properties.[15] Borrowers gained again in 1892 when the interest rate was dropped once more, this time to 4½%. This move came because of 'the diminution in the earning power of Money, and to meet the times'.[16] It boosted advances by over half in the following year and enabled a subsequent increase of ½% in the rate of interest to borrowers. This was above that gained by the Society on its deposits in the bank and it led to a more optimistic assessment of the future despite a drastic drop in income from almost £75,000 in 1893 to just over £56,000 in 1894.[17]

The Liberator Crash and Star-Bowkett Societies

It is likely that this precipitous fall was associated as much with the 'Liberator Crash' of late 1892 as it was with bad trading conditions. Although it had operated as supposedly the largest building society in the country, the Liberator 'had little in common with *bona fide* Building Societies except its name'.[18]

Holloway Bank, West Bromwich, about 1905. (with the permission of Sandwell Community History and Archives Service)

Notice to members of the West Bromwich Permanent Benefit Building Society, 6 June 1898.

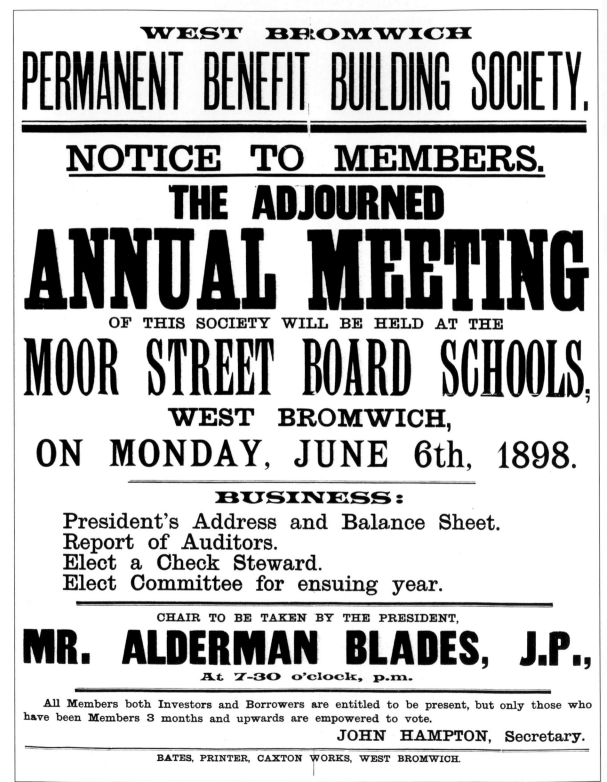

WEST BROMWICH
PERMANENT BENEFIT BUILDING SOCIETY.

NOTICE TO MEMBERS.

THE ADJOURNED
ANNUAL MEETING

OF THIS SOCIETY WILL BE HELD AT THE

MOOR STREET BOARD SCHOOLS,

WEST BROMWICH,

ON MONDAY, JUNE 6th, 1898.

BUSINESS:

President's Address and Balance Sheet.
Report of Auditors.
Elect a Check Steward.
Elect Committee for ensuing year.

CHAIR TO BE TAKEN BY THE PRESIDENT,

MR. ALDERMAN BLADES, J.P.,

At 7-30 o'clock, p.m.

All Members both Investors and Borrowers are entitled to be present, but only those who have been Members 3 months and upwards are empowered to vote.

JOHN HAMPTON, Secretary.

BATES, PRINTER, CAXTON WORKS, WEST BROMWICH.

Dominated by J.S. Balfour, it was used by him to provide mortgages for estates bought by property companies which he either owned or was associated with deeply. The interest on these loans was paid with further loans from the Liberator with no additional securities given. Such double dealings were hidden cleverly from the society's shareholders, who continued to trust Balfour because of his Non-Conformist and temperance background. Then on 2 September 1892 his bank, the London and General, suspended payments and it became clear that the Liberator did not have the funds to provide payments to members and depositors wishing to make withdrawals. The society was wound up and Balfour was later sentenced to fourteen years' imprisonment for fraud.[19]

Those who suffered most from the crash were 'poor and helpless people' and there can be no doubt that building societies in general suffered from bad publicity. This was acknowledged by the committee of the West Bromwich. In its report of 12 June 1893 it stated that 'from the failure of several building societies during the past year, a rude shock has been given to that class of Investors who avail themselves of the advantages of Building Societies, in order to become their own Landlords or to make some provision against bad times and old age'. Withdrawals were nearly 50% more than the preceding year, although 'no inconvenience has been experienced on that account'. Declaring itself an 'old established and well tried Building Society' the West Bromwich hoped that its high standing would ensure public confidence.[21] Overall it did and by 1896 receipts had swept back to the £70,000 mark.[22]

That year another Building Societies Act was passed. It aimed to close loopholes in the 1874 legislation and prevent another Liberator-style scandal. Accordingly, all incorporated societies were required to specify in their rules the terms on which all shares were issued and the way in which losses would be met; to ensure that one of their auditors was an accountant; to strengthen the auditor's certificate; and to make a return of amounts due on mortgages – in aggregate for certain groups up to £5,000 and individually for those above that limit. Additionally the Registrar of Building Societies was empowered either to allow a member to inspect a society's books or to appoint an inspector to do so; to suspend or cancel registrations and in certain situations to dissolve a society; and to publish details of the annual returns of the societies. Other sections ensured that returns had to be made on properties which had been in the possession of a society for more than a year through the default of the mortgagors, and on mortgages more than twelve months in arrears. Finally, in a move against 'Promoter' societies, balloting for advances was prohibited in new societies.

These organisations had been initiated by T.E. Bowkett, a radical doctor who was fervent in his belief that building societies needed to reach out to both the middle ranks of the working class and the poor. Realising that neither group could afford the dues of building societies he proposed a solution. One hundred people would form a society and each pay 9½d a week into a common fund. At the end of the year the society would have £205 16s 8d and members would draw lots for an interest-free advance of £200 to be secured by a mortgage on a house.

The winner would carry on paying his or her subscriptions and add to them 8s a week so that the loan could be cleared in ten years. In this way after eleven months another draw could be made. With each winner the time between draws was lessened and within thirty-one years all members would have received an advance. In another ten years the last mortgage would have been repaid, and the total of subscriptions, less expenses and plus fines, would be repaid to the members.

Bowkett's ideas were taken up by Richard Star, who devised a plan for shortening the life of draw societies and so make them more appealing. The first Star-Bowkett Society was formed in 1862 and by the 1890s they were widespread. Star gave advice to each new society which followed his outlines, and charged the secretary for doing so. He was paid also by those who were appointed as surveyor and solicitor. Star's rules made sure that such officers had security of tenure so that they could make money from their positions. Because of his success as a promoter, others followed his example – modifying his rules to allow them to avoid his copyrights. Amongst them were the Model, Self Help, Richmond, and Perfect Thrift Societies. All of them were controversial. Their supporters may have seen them as encouraging frugality but their detractors decried them for destroying the virtue of thrift. The arguments of opponents were sustained by the changing nature of the subscribers to promoter societies. Increasingly they attracted not only those seeking a house but those looking for a quick cash prize. This association with gambling meant that legislators were willing to move against the promoters. Thus, although existing societies were not banned by the 1894 Act, their future demise was ensured by the prevention of new ones from forming. Simply this was because they operated on the terminating principle.[23]

The Improving Affairs of the West Bromwich Building Society

In the wake of the 1894 Act, the West Bromwich continued to operate as an unincorporated body with five trustees and it consolidated its financial position despite the continuing difficulty of 'placing out all the Money on good securities'.[24] With too much cash lying idle and mortgagors reluctant to come forward, the Society had little option but to reduce the interest of its 3½% depositors to 3%. Three-quarters of them accepted this move, with the remainder withdrawing their savings. In another attempt to counter the nation-wide problems, the West Bromwich resolved in 1898 'that all borrowing Members on the Books at the next annual clearing night shall have out of the profits made during the coming year a Bonus of ½% on those charged at 4½% interest'. In effect this lowered their charge to 4% compared to the 4½% interest of new borrowers.[25] The bonus was carried on in the next year, although the valuation of properties was now to be borne by the borrower.[26] To ensure that savers would not be pushed from the Society, the bonus was reduced to ¼% in 1900 so that the committee could 'declare a higher rate of profit to the Investing Members'.[27]

Advertisement for West Bromwich Permanent Benefit Building Society, about 1900.

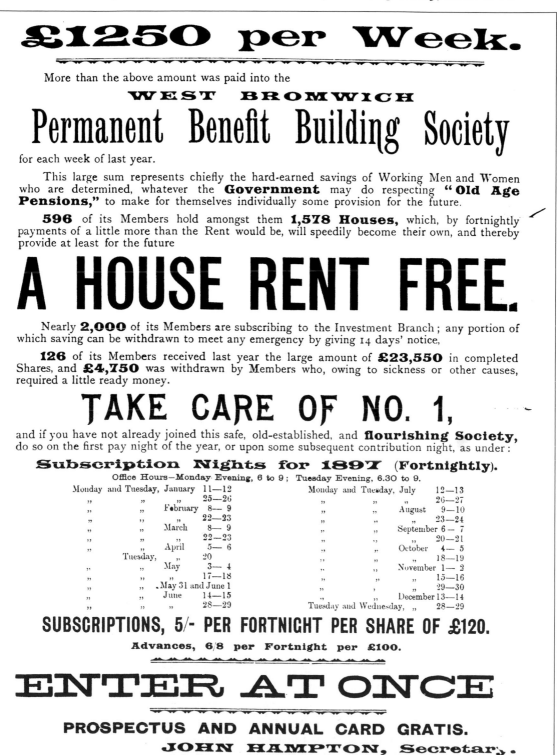

£1250 per Week.

More than the above amount was paid into the

WEST BROMWICH
Permanent Benefit Building Society

for each week of last year.

This large sum represents chiefly the hard-earned savings of Working Men and Women who are determined, whatever the **Government** may do respecting **"Old Age Pensions,"** to make for themselves individually some provision for the future.

596 of its Members hold amongst them **1,578 Houses,** which, by fortnightly payments of a little more than the Rent would be, will speedily become their own, and thereby provide at least for the future

A HOUSE RENT FREE.

Nearly **2,000** of its Members are subscribing to the Investment Branch; any portion of which saving can be withdrawn to meet any emergency by giving 14 days' notice,

126 of its Members received last year the large amount of **£23,550** in completed Shares, and **£4,750** was withdrawn by Members who, owing to sickness or other causes, required a little ready money.

TAKE CARE OF NO. 1,

and if you have not already joined this safe, old-established, and **flourishing Society,** do so on the first pay night of the year, or upon some subsequent contribution night, as under:

Subscription Nights for 1897 (Fortnightly).

Office Hours—Monday Evening, 6 to 9; Tuesday Evening, 6.30 to 9.

Monday and Tuesday,		January	11—12	Monday and Tuesday,		July	12—13
,,	,,	,,	25—26	,,	,,	,,	26—27
,,	,,	February	8— 9	,,	,,	August	9—10
,,	,,	,,	22—23	,,	,,	,,	23—24
,,	,,	March	8— 9	,,	,,	September 6 — 7	
,,	,,	,,	22—23	,,	,,	,,	20—21
,,	,,	April	5— 6	,,	,,	October	4— 5
	Tuesday,	,,	20	,,	,,	,,	18—19
,,	,,	May	3— 4	,,	,,	November 1 — 2	
,,	,,	,,	17—18	,,	,,	,,	15—16
,,	,,	May 31 and June 1		,,	,,	,,	29—30
,,	,,	June	14—15	,,	,,	December 13—14	
,,	,,	,,	28—29	Tuesday and Wednesday,		,,	28—29

SUBSCRIPTIONS, 5/- PER FORTNIGHT PER SHARE OF £120.

Advances, 6/8 per Fortnight per £100.

ENTER AT ONCE

PROSPECTUS AND ANNUAL CARD GRATIS.
JOHN HAMPTON, Secretary.

J. B. ROUND, JUNCTION PRINTING WORKS, WEST BROMWICH.

The early years of the new century heralded a marked improvement in affairs. In particular, the increased value of money resulted in a 'very great demand for twenty eight houses'.[28] By 1905, there were 746 borrowing members on the books, 150 more than in 1896. Of the former, 79% were people who had received advances of less than £500 – almost the same proportion as nine years previously; another 18% had loans of between £500 and £1,000 – again comparable with the earlier date; and only twenty-eight folk had mortgages worth between £1,000 and £2,000.[29] These figures make plain that West Bromwich had successfully come through an arduous period for building societies, one in which some had failed and others, like the Smethwick Building Society, had been preyed upon by cheats. In 1883 the secretary of that institution was accused of forgery and embezzlement to the sum of about £2,000.[30] The West Bromwich was never tainted by such a disgrace and unsurprisingly in the good year of 1905 a measure of self-congratulation was evident in the annual report:[31]

> . . . your Committee is assured that the prudent course the West Bromwich Building Society has followed throughout its career has never resulted in any diminution in public favour, but entirely and substantially the reverse; so we may be very certain that the continued preservation of a high tone in the conduct of its business will serve it in good stead in the future. The splendid fruit of able minds and diligent hands which shaped its early destinies, the Society is today as then committed to the guidance of strong men who recognise to the full the dignity and importance of their trust. And while that spirit animates the administration of this Society the fortunes which await it in the future can hardly fail to be less gratifying than those which have attended its operations in the past.[32]

Extolling 'mutual self help' and 'the direct encouragement to thrift' as its salient features, the West Bromwich substantially increased its receipts in 1907 from £71,850 17s 6d to £80,409.[33] A year later it advanced the record sum of £53,935 on mortgages. This debt was spread over 814 properties, an increase of sixty four on the previous year, and averaged a mortgage of £252 on each house. In every instance, the Society held the first mortgage. By this date, investors who made regular subscriptions were receiving compound interest of 4⅜%.[34] The Society's appeal to investors was emphasised in 1910 when it was revealed that it had 456 depositors' accounts and 2,136 investors' accounts compared with 830 borrowers' accounts. This situation led the committee to draw attention to the ability of the West Bromwich 'to make immediate Advances on approved securities in any part of England, and appeal for assistance in getting to work forthwith the large amount now in the Bankers' hands'.[35] The next year, in 1911, the building society movement was rocked yet again when the Birkbeck collapsed. This society had barely managed to survive the crash of the Liberator, and similarly it was brought down because it did not adhere to sound building society practice. From its beginnings in 1851 the Birkbeck had followed a policy of investing at least three-quarters of its deposits in consols (government and other securities without a maturity date) or other convertible securities. This decision ensured that it would act more as a bank and indeed by the early 1890s, it was regarded as the sixth-largest such institution in the country. Its failure was brought about by the decline in the market value of government securities, which meant that it had not the resources to survive 'abnormally high withdrawals'.[36] The failure of the Birkbeck reinforced those societies which believed in the core objectives of the building society movement, and it is significant that no building society has gone bust since the Second World War.

Perhaps insulated from the fall of the Birkbeck because of its careful management and high local reputation, the West Bromwich continued to draw in large deposits – in spite of its best efforts to lend more on sound houses. By 1914, as Europe was poised to plunge into the horrors of the Great War, its receipts had reached £87,828 – a record figure.[37] Obviously, the enlarging funds of the West Bromwich were accompanied by increased running costs. When it had been set up, only £11 17s 10d had been outlayed on books, stationery, printing, advertising, postage and enrolling rules; whilst in its first two years of existence, just under £16 had been spent on the rent, cleaning and heating of the Paradise Street Methodist School Rooms, a tea party, and the salary of the secretary. At £4 a year, it is obvious that this was a part-time position.[38] Expenses increased noticeably in succeeding years as the Society became more extensive in its dealings. By 1864 they included payments to a steward, sub-treasurer and outside auditors; bank commission; surveyors' charges; printing; and postage. Anxious to pursue 'a policy of wise economy' the committee stressed that at 1¼% of income the management of the Society was moderate 'and will bear favourable comparison with any similar Institution'.[39] It did. In 1871 the expenses of the Sun Permanent Society were put at 3-4% of turnover, whilst those of the London and General Society were about 2%.[40]

The growth of the Society meant that the offices in Lower High Street soon became 'most inadequate' and in 1866 it was noted that better accommodation was needed.[41] Because of the 'calamities that caused a fearful stagnation of trade' the following year, the matter was put in abeyance until 1869.[42] That year, a lease was taken 'on more commodious Premises' and new offices were built for £181 6s 1d – towards which the lessors paid £42. The balance was to be written off over a term of fourteen years.[43] Located at 298 High Street, the premises were rented at £30 a year – £10 more than that of the previous offices.[44] They were used until 1879 when another move was precipitated by the ongoing development of the Society's business. A house and premises were bought from Messrs. Duncalfe and Evans at 301, High Street. Plans for new offices and a fire-proof room for 'the safe custody of Books, Deeds and Documents' were drawn up by the Society's surveyor.[45] Costing £3,389 10s 10d to erect and fit out, the headquarters itself fittingly looked as if it could have been a Methodist Chapel, distinctive as it was with one storey and a pitched roof.[46] That sum included money spent on the secretary's house and the purchase of surplus land.

In the report of 1891, it was recorded that the site at 301, High Street had been purchased not from Messrs. Duncalfe and Evans but from Mr. W.F.H. Whitehouse, and that it consisted only of land and not premises. It was added that between the new offices and the High Street Congregational Chapel there was a valuable piece of property which 'it was supposed might realize a high price at some future time'. The trustees of the chapel believed that they were entitled to a right of light over this land – a claim disputed by the West Bromwich. So as to 'assert the Society's right to the free use and enjoyment' of the plot the committee authorised the erection of a boundary wall. Unfortunately this action caused acrimony. The Society responded by suggesting that if the chapel's trustees paid a nominal acknowledgement of 1s a year then the West Bromwich would covenant that during its existence 'no building should be erected to obscure the Chapel lights'. The offer was refused and, after legal proceedings were started, a High Court judge found against the building society. At more than £357, the legal costs were heavy, especially considering that the next year an agreement was reached whereby a building line was drawn between the chapel and the Society's property.[48]

Throughout the early years at the Paradise Street Methodist School Rooms, prospectuses, rules and information were available from the secretary on alternate Mondays between 7.00 p.m. and 9.00 p.m., whilst meetings for members were also held fortnightly between these hours.[49] There is no information as to the hours of business at the offices either in the Lower High Street or at 298, High Street. However from 1902, the purpose-built premises at 301, High Street were open every weekday for members to make enquiries and obtain information. Additionally on alternate Mondays and Tuesdays, the staff would be available during the day and the night 'as before for the purpose of receiving subscriptions'.[50] The new hours were satisfactory 'and largely removed the congestion and inconvenience which had been experienced'.[51] In 1909 the *Prospectus* indicated that the office hours were 10.00 a.m. until 1.30 p.m. and 3.00 p.m. until 4.30 p.m. each day. The exceptions were Wednesdays, when business ended at 1.00 p.m. and re-started for two hours from 6.30 p.m.; and Saturdays, when the staff were present from 9.30 a.m. until 12 noon. Subscriptions could now be paid each Monday between 6.00 p.m. and 9.00 p.m., and each Tuesday from 6.30 p.m. until 9.00 p.m.[52]

Running the West Bromwich Building Society

The increased business which necessitated longer opening hours also led to a more sophisticated approach to the running of the West Bromwich. This development was given added impetus by burgeoning local bye-laws which related to building and national legislation which required certain organisations to employ professionals. From the beginnings of the Society, two auditors signed the balance sheets which accompanied the annual reports – but it appears that they were performing a voluntary role until 1857 when a payment of £2 2s was recorded for their services.[53] Because the auditors changed so often, it also seems that their duty was carried on by members. There are indications of this situation changing in 1883 when Grove Shaw became one of the auditors. He held his position for fourteen years, and from 1890 his name was followed by the initials F.S.A.[54] Three years previously he had been joined as co-auditor by Clement Keys, a chartered accountant. He was still in office in 1914, accompanied by his partner of sixteen years, George Coleman F.C.A.[55]

Stone Cross Inn, West Bromwich, about 1905.
(with the permission of Sandwell Community History and Archives Service)

The *1909 Prospectus* of the West Bromwich emphasised the Society's financial stability and its 'character for fair and liberal dealing with its Members'. This feature was enhanced by the involvement of professionals, as was made plain. It was stated that the accounts of the Society were audited by two qualified accountants and that 'members are supplied with a copy of the Balance Sheet and a clear statement of their accounts each year'. The prospectus also indicated that the West Bromwich had its own surveyor, who 'by special arrangement only charges Members 2½% on the outlay for buildings (i.e. half the usual charge)'. His task was to make plans, prepare the specification, procure tenders from competent builders and submit the plans to the local authority. Once these were approved, the surveyor would supervise the building work, 'and thereby save the Member much trouble and ensure the well-doing of the work'. He would be paid by the Society upon his certificate as the work proceeded.[56] For many years until his resignation in 1902 the surveyor was Thomas Rollason.[57] His office was also in the High Street, as were those of the two solicitors of the Society – A. Caddick and William Bache. Similarly the West Bromwich made its own deposits with the Metropolitan Bank at its branch in the High Street.[58]

Surveyor's charges were mentioned from the annual report of 1855. By that date, James P. Sharp was also signing the balance sheet in his capacity as secretary.[59] Four years later he had been replaced by John Hampton, who had been one of the auditors in the year before. It is apparent that he was a full-time employee with a weekly income of 34 shillings.[60] This was a standard sum for a lower-middle-class clerk and put his earnings slightly, but definitely above, all but the best-paid of the working class. In the succeeding years, his wages rose sharply, and by 1872, he was earning over £4 a week.[61] The next year, the accounts revealed that he had assistants.[62] John Hampton 'served the Society faithfully for many years' and died in office, as was recorded in 1902.[63] He was succeeded for a short time by Thomas Hampton, who died before the Fifty-Fourth Annual Report of 1903. By this date James Coleman was in office. Interestingly he shared the surname of one of the auditors and had been treasurer until his new appointment.[64] The position of treasurer itself had been mentioned first in 1860 when a testimonial of £17 5s had been made to the person who had voluntarily carried on the duty since the founding of the Society.[65]

It seems highly probable that James Coleman the secretary and George Coleman the auditor were related to the George Coleman who had been one of the founders of the West Bromwich. His death was mentioned in 1882 when a tribute of respect was made to his memory.[66] For several years previously he had acted as a trustee, as had another of the founders, John Silvester. Named as Enoch at the start of the Society, he 'rejoiced greatly in the growth and the prosperity' of the West Bromwich. Although active as a manufacturer 'he was one of those English worthies, who find time to help forward projects which have for their object the social advancement of their fellow men. To do good while he lived was with him a rule of conduct; and as a practical philanthropist, he strove manfully to do his part to leaving the world better than he found it'.[67]

Silvester had been appointed a trustee on 10 April 1854 along with Samuel Withers. Then describing himself as a gentleman, Withers is the only other founder about whom there is mention in the records of the West Bromwich after the original meeting.[68] Two of his descendants have traced his life and by 1861 he was living in a large house at 75, Birmingham Road with his widowed mother and sister and two unmarried brothers. Described in the census of that year once more as a glass cutter, a decade later he is recorded a rent collector and agent. Now residing at 19 Bagnall Street, with his widowed sister and a housekeeper, 'one can sense that he had made the transition to a middle-class solidity'. At his death he left £7,000, which provided an annuity to his only surviving brother, Thomas. His granddaughter always maintained that 'the building society money' kept her grandfather in comfort and educated his four youngest boys.[69]

It is unlikely that Withers did gain significantly from his involvement with the West Bromwich. The office of trustee was unpaid, whilst when he acted as treasurer in 1868 he would have received only £7 7s for what in effect was a part-time and poorly remunerated office.[70] What is more probable is that his active involvement in the affairs of the Society reflected his move from the working class into 'middle-class solidity'. At the same time, the West Bromwich itself was becoming more of a middle-class institution. This is reflected in the occupations of the trustees. Of the others elected in 1854, Allan Watton was a gentleman,

A share certificate, 1869.

Thomas Icke was a currier and Robert Spear Hudson was a chemist. In the succeeding years no trustee could be regarded as working class. This absence is highlighted by the occupations of the trustees in 1914: John Marston was a grocer; Edwin Hazel was a retired engineer; Thomas Whitehurst was a chief superintendent of police; George Garratt was a provision merchant; and Josiah Guest, was an ironfounder.[71] The West Bromwich was not singular in the transformation of its leadership. In 1872 the Royal Commission on Friendly Societies reported that the growth of building societies had 'altogether changed their character' and had tended to throw them more and more 'into the hands of the middle classes and secure to them its benefits'.[72] Notwithstanding this comment, it would be unfair to suggest that the West Bromwich in particular had completely thrown off its working-class origins. It is true that as early as 1861 the Society had advertised itself as offering facilities for 'the safe investment of money – alike to the advantage of the Capitalist, the Tradesman, and the Working Man', yet it did not forsake its working-class members.[73] Two years later the committee still sought to render the Society 'more extensively useful, among the breadwinners of Westbromwich and district' and to draw in 'new blood'. It actively solicited the co-operation of its members for that purpose, explaining that:

> It may not be generally known that the price per day of a pint of ale and paper of tobacco, in other words, about fourpence per day paid into the funds of this Society, would entitle a depositing member to receive £120 at the expiration of about eleven years; and a member who built or bought House Property in a judicious manner, the same trifling rates of contribution, in addition to the rental, would place him in even better a position.[74]

The Influence of Reuben Farley

From its inception, the West Bromwich had been imbued with the beliefs of those who sought to improve the position of the working class. House ownership was a major means to that end. With power increasingly vested in a middle-class leadership, the attitudes of the Society changed in a subtle way. No longer was the aim that of working-class self-advancement. Now it was the reform of the working class through the influence of the middle class. Increasingly it was believed that bad housing fostered immorality and bad habits. Thus membership of a building society, savings and house purchase were seen as ways whereby working-class people could be improved for the benefit of the state. This national preoccupation permeated the report of 1866. It was proclaimed that housing with proper sanitary arrangements, better drainage and ventilation, and a greater number of cubic feet of space for sleeping accommodation would lead to 'habits of temperance and cleanliness', the lowering of death rates and the fostering of the virtues of purity and chastity.[75]

Alderman Reuben Farley, first President of West Bromwich Permanent Benefit Building Society, 1849-1898, and the first Mayor of West Bromwich.

Almost twenty years later it was thought 'difficult to overestimate the good influence which this Society has exercised in improving the habits of thrift and frugality in the Black Country', and it was hoped that 'long may it continue its career of wise and beneficient influence'.[76] Yet for all that, the West Bromwich believed it had a role as a missionary, it was not as antagonistic towards the working class as were most middle-class organisations. In 1874 the committee was concerned by the fact that locally 'the paralysed state of the staple trades has been aggravated by labour disputes'. Unhappily there was a colliers' strike 'of great magnitude' and the question was posed that 'surely the time is not too far distant when all labour disputes may be amicably settled without having recourse to lock-outs and strikes. To accomplish this there needs a general diffusion of sound economic knowledge upon all questions affecting Labour and Capital'.[77] In keeping with this conciliatory tone, in 1881 it was explained that the Society 'is based upon sound principles of equity, with a determination on the part of the Executive to do what is just and honest between man and man'.[78]

This statement bears the mark of a remarkable man, Reuben Farley. Although not one of the founders of the Society, he was one of the two members who audited the balance sheet which accompanied the earliest document pertaining to the West Bromwich – the Second Annual Report (31 May 1851). He did so again the next year, and, from 1858 until his retirement in 1897 he signed each annual report as President. Born in 1825 just across the borders of West Bromwich in Great Bridge, Tipton, he was the son of a mining engineer who died when Farley was five. He himself became a coalmaster 'and by hard work and that marked business ability which has distinguished all his undertakings' he made his business successful.[79] In 1861, when he was already President of the West Bromwich, Farley and his brother-in-law, George Taylor, bought a foundry. This also prospered and in the succeeding years Farley became chairman of Fellows, Moreton and Clayton Ltd., the largest canal carriers in England; chairman of Edward Danks Ltd., boiler makers of Oldbury; a director of the Hamstead Colliery Company; and an active force in the Sandwell Park Colliery.

Reuben Farley's business exploits were matched by his accomplishments in public life. He was typical of those powerful manufacturers who passionately believed that they owed a duty to the localities from which they had made their fortunes. If Bradford had its Titus Salt, Manchester its John Bright and Birmingham its Joseph Chamberlain then West Bromwich was fortunate to have its Reuben Farley. From when he was a young man he 'unceasingly identified himself with all the principal movements having for their object the progress and well-being of the town and its inhabitants'. As a member of the Board of Guardians, President of the West Bromwich, a county magistrate, chairman of the Improvement Commissioners, and member of the first School Board locally Farley had 'by his ability, energy, and conscientious discharge of duty, together with his unvarying courtesy of demeanour, acquitted himself to the approbation of his fellow townsmen of all classes, without distinction of creed or party'.[80] Under his leadership of the commissioners West Bromwich obtained its own gas works and was provided with

The Farley Clock Tower at Carter's Green,
West Bromwich, 1952.
(with permission of Birmingham Evening Mail)

The historic Oak House, West Bromwich, 1988.
(with permission of Birmingham Evening Mail)

major civic structures such as the Town Hall, Free Library, Market Hall and baths; and it was he who was instrumental in persuading its owner to give Dartmouth Park to the town – and if he 'had done nothing more than this his name would be revered by every one in West Bromwich'.[81]

When the town was incorporated in 1882 Farley was elected unanimously as mayor – indeed no other name was even suggested for the position. He continued to act vigorously on behalf of his people, donating land in Greets Green for a park named after him and bestowing the Oak House Museum and Recreation Ground to West Bromwich. In 1896 he became the first Freeman of West Bromwich, whilst his fellow citizens put up a clock tower to show their appreciation of his services on their behalf.[82] The death in 1899 of 'Our Grand Old Man' was seen as a blow for the whole of West Bromwich.[83] The position he gained as a self-made man was 'entirely due to his meritorious conduct, integrity and ability'. As a moderate Liberal and a keen Anglican, Farley stood out for his 'high sense of honour', 'stainless character' and 'steady zeal in the interests of religion, morality and benevolence'.[84] Not least amongst his achievements was guiding the rapid growth of the West Bromwich so that it had 'a firm hold upon the public'.[85] His tremendous contribution was acknowledged in 1898 when he retired as President. The annual meeting resolved unanimously to 'tender him its grateful thanks for the labour and attention he has given to the Society as its President for more than 40 years; they regret very much that while his interest and confidence in the Society continues unabated, his numerous engagements and advancing years constrain him to resign a position which he has honoured by his constant and careful attention'.[86]

The Society was affected deeply by Reuben Farley's death, as it had been earlier that year by the passing of Thomas Icke, 'our much respected Senior Trustee and Treasurer'.[87] This left Josiah Guest as the longest-serving trustee, followed by Brownlow William Blades. Elected in 1884, Blades had begun his working life as a brickmaker in West Bromwich. Through 'his temperance and thrifty habits' he saved enough money to join his employer as a partner. Later the sole proprietor of a large blue brick works in Tipton, Blades was keenly involved in the affairs both of that town and of West Bromwich, where he lived. A staunch Wesleyan and an ardent supporter of religious and political liberty, throughout the Black Country he was known as the Apostle of Temperance. In 1861 he was joined in business by his son, John Horton Blades. By the early 1890s the younger Blades and his brother were running the brick works at the Swan Village Estate. It was a sizeable undertaking and in less than four years it supplied Birmingham Corporation alone with over twelve million blue paving bricks.[88]

Like Farley, Blades was a public-spirited man. Formerly a member of the Improvement Commissioners, he was elected a councillor when West Bromwich was incorporated and in 1883 he became chairman of the Markets, Baths and Park Committee – a position he held for many years. Regarded as an 'earnest and painstaking member', his importance was recognised in 1885 when he was

Alderman John Horton Blades, second President of West Bromwich Permanent Benefit Building Society, 1898-1916, and the first MP for West Bromwich.

made an alderman. The same year he was elected as the first Member of Parliament for West Bromwich. A Liberal, he was congratulated by his Conservative opponents 'on the gentlemanly manner in which he conducted the fight'. Although he did not stand for re-election, John Blades remained a powerful figure in West Bromwich. In particular, he took an interest in education and was secretary of 'one of the most flourishing denominational schools in the district, the Great Bridge Wesleyan'. He had two other over-riding concerns: first that the 'saving grace of temperance' could abolish nearly all the poverty and misery 'endured by the masses'; and second the 'advantages accruing from thrifty habits'. Both beliefs led him to express 'a deep interest in the welfare of the working classes' and to an association with the Birmingham Mutual Benefit Society and the Rechabites – a temperance friendly society.[89]

With such attitudes and with such an imposing presence locally, Blades was a natural choice as President in 1898. His reports lack the grittiness and fervour of those of Farley, but they are fuller in their discussion of the financial affairs of the Society. At the same time they regularly assert the positive role of the West Bromwich in 'improving the habit of thrift in the Black Country' and in providing for better homes 'without coming on the rates'.[90] He made his last report on 10 June 1915, and once again he pointed out 'the necessity for economy and thrift'.[91] John Horton Blades died in April 1916. In his obituary it was maintained that under 'his able control' that 'valuable Society' the West Bromwich had made 'such headway that at several annual meetings now record years of business' had been remarked upon. His successor was to preside over even more success for the Society.

Chapter 3:

The Home of Thrift, 1914-38

The Effects of The First World War

By the outbreak of the First World War, the building society movement appeared to have overcome the problems caused by the failures of prominent societies and had regained public confidence. But the demands of a war economy imposed new pressures. Interest rates were raised and restrictions were placed upon the rights of home owners and mortgagors. Moreover, from 1915 investors were drawn towards the higher returns offered by the government on war loans.[1] Imbued by a spirit of patriotism, the West Bromwich was like many societies in that it ensured that 'every facility has been given to Members and Depositors wishing to withdraw their money for the purpose of investing with the Government'. In order to meet the subsequent large amount of withdrawals, the Society built up a significant level of surplus funds – in itself bolstered from 1915 by the decision to restrict advances.[2]

John Marston, third President of West Bromwich Permanent Benefit Building Society, 1921.

Unlike some of its fellows, the West Bromwich did not discontinue mortgages altogether, although it did raise the interest rate for new borrowers to 5% because of the increased income tax 'which the Society pays on behalf of its Members and Depositors'. It also ended the bonus to existing mortgagors, meaning that they now paid 4½%.[3] With the death of Alderman Blades, that year's report was signed by Councillor Edward Arnold, the recently-elected vice-President. In 1917 the office of President was taken by John Marston, a grocer in Lyng Lane who had been a trustee for a decade. One of his first tasks was to liaise with The Building Societies Association over the issue of property tax, and 'through the good efforts' of that body the amount paid by the West Bromwich was 'much less than anticipated'.[4]

Although incomes were rising nationally, the economic circumstances caused by the war meant that overall building society assets went up only slightly from £66.2 million in 1914 to £68.5 million four years later. These figures compared poorly with the assets of £76 million in 1910, before the Birkbeck failure. Such statistics have led to the interpretation that the war 'had confirmed and prolonged the already long period of relative stagnation from 1875 to 1914 compared with the vigour of the early and mid-Victorian period'.[5] The West Bromwich itself does not fit into this analysis as it appears to have fared better than the movement as a whole. In 1893 its receipts had been £52,831; by 1914 they had swollen to £87,828; and, by 1919, they had reached £105,063. At the same time membership had expanded to 4,400 whilst assets had burgeoned to over a quarter-of-a-million pounds.[6] Two years later, it was noted with pride that out of 1,370 societies nationally, the West Bromwich was one of only twenty

Alderman Edward Arnold J.P., fourth President of West Bromwich Permanent Benefit Building Society, 1922-7.

seven which had a membership of over 5,000.[7] It seems that the high reputation of a society embedded deeply within its locality had gained it custom at a time when bigger and more metropolitan societies were treading water.

The 'remarkable progress of the Society' was stressed by President John Marston in 1918. He proclaimed that it had never been in a sounder position and the 'war had not adversely affected' its work.

> they were able to record the greatest progress since its foundation. The receipts were more, the membership was more and the assets were more. During the year they advanced £42,285 on mortgage, sufficient to provide 140 houses and to accommodate 700 people. With the housing question occupying such a prominent position in all parts of the country, he was sure they would be interested to know that since the establishment of the Society, they had advanced on mortgage £1,561,435, sufficient to accommodate over 26,000 people, or over a third of the population of West Bromwich, assuming the advance had been £300.[8]

The Expansion in House Building and Home Ownership

This housing question was one of the major priorities of the coalition government led by Lloyd George. Like so many members of the upper and middle- classes, ministers had been amazed by the patriotic fervour of working-class men and women during the war. They had come forward enthusiastically to fight and work for a country from which they had gained little, living as they mostly did in insanitary and decrepit housing. Affected deeply by this commitment to the nation, the authorities exclaimed that once the war was ended they would build a 'Land Fit for Heroes' in which everyone would live in 'Homes Fit for Heroes'.

As early as 1917 an Advisory Housing panel had been set up and an appeal had been made to local authorities. This made the point that private enterprise would be unable to deal swiftly and successfully with the massive house-building programme which would be needed when peace came. The next year, there was a momentous change of policy by the government when it agreed to offer substantial financial aid to councils which would construct municipal houses. This shift had a rapid impact and in 1918 Alderman Arnold, vice-President of the West Bromwich, mentioned 'that the Corporation had purchased the Tantany estate, and added that in connection with any scheme which might be undertaken in West Bromwich, they might rely upon it that Alderman Kenrick would do anything he could to further the interests of the Building Society'.[9]

During the inter-war years, councils throughout the land did erect tens of thousands of houses to rent. Obviously there was a fear amongst building societies that such a development would hinder their operations. As it was, they gained greatly simply because private-house construction outstripped that by councils. This trend occurred in spite of the severe economic troubles of the 1920s and the Depression, which blighted the lives of large numbers of people from 1929 until rearmament in the late 1930s. It cannot be denied that during these 'devil's decades' job losses were heavy, especially in the staple industries of cotton, coal, iron and steel. In areas associated with these trades many men and their families

Indenture of Mortgage between Enoch John Smith and the Trustees of West Bromwich Permanent Benefit Building Society, 28 July 1914.

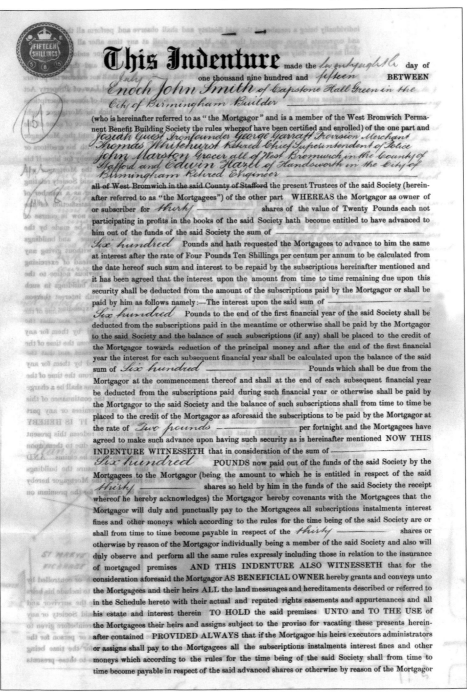

were plunged into poverty. Ill health, bad housing and hunger marches were a reality for too many Britons, yet others prospered. There was expansion in newer manufactures like that of processed foods, whilst there was a growth in the employment of clerks. Indeed, the majority of those in work were more affluent than ever before. The cost of living was falling, real wages were rising and the birth rate was dropping. These circumstances led to a greater disposable income for most regularly employed members of the working and middle classes. Their spending power fuelled domestic demand for electrical goods, cars and houses.

West Bromwich was a microcosm of England in the inter-war years. Coal mining and iron-ore extraction had been contracting since 1900, a process which led to long dole queues locally. Moreover, the town did not gain as quickly from the newer manufactures as did Birmingham, Smethwick and Oldbury. Still, it had a wider industrial base than that of most other Black Country towns. As well as spring and tube makers, ironfounders, drop forgers and other metal manufacturers, West Bromwich was a centre of printing with firms such as Kenrick and Jefferson; it had a leading office supplier in Manifoldia, and it boasted the headquarters of one of West Midlands' best-known grocers – George Mason's. Consequently, West Bromwich did not suffer as much unemployment as did Cradley, Bilston, Dudley and Wednesbury.[10] The town was marked out as representative of the nation by one other feature – the development of new council estates. Under the Housing and Town Planning Act of 1919 and successive legislation the corporation built houses at Tantany, Charlemont, Friar Park, Hambletts, Hateley Heath, Hall Green, Greets Green, Marsh Lane and Hamstead. There was also widespread action by private house builders in the Great Barr area.[11]

The idea of 'buying your own house' had been invigorated by the Housing Act of 1923. Associated with Neville Chamberlain of Birmingham, the minister for housing policy, it encouraged councils to lend money to enable private house purchase; it supported building societies by making mortgages easier; and it provided a subsidy for dwellings erected by both private builders and local authorities. This legislation was accompanied by falling building costs which saw the price of a three bedroom house without a parlour drop from £930 in August 1920 to £436 in March 1922.[12] House purchase was further stimulated in the mid-1930s by the 'extraordinary cheapness of money' which led all building societies to reduce their rates of interest.[13]

The West Bromwich was particularly well poised to attract the new members who wanted to own their home. Emerging strongly from the First World War, it strode forward confidently in peacetime and came to be regarded as one of 'the best-managed and most flourishing building societies in the country'.[14] By 1927, it had 7,819 members, 1,237 depositors and total assets of £543,186. This consolidated its position as a major society but still left it far behind the front-runners of the movement, like the Halifax Equitable Benefit which boasted total assets of £11 million.[15] Still the West Bromwich made noteworthy progress and between 1919 and 1938, on only three occasions were records for annual

A share certificate, 1927.

receipts not broken. So impressive was the Society's expansion that in 1935 it
was reported as 'phenomenal'. That year's receipts were £1.3 million, whilst the
assets were recorded as well over £2 million. The vice-President, William H.
Nock, commented that:

> they had always endeavoured to help the owner-occupier, and the balance-
> sheet showed that their efforts in that direction had been appreciated. They
> had always tried, too, to deal fairly as between investors and borrowers, and
> this was also shown to be appreciated by the large number of clients they had
> outside the borough. There had been many wonderful records set up during
> the King's Jubilee reign, and it was pleasing to know that the Building
> Society had shared in this progress during this period. In the last twenty-five
> years the Society's accounts had grown by 589 per cent., the receipts being
> 1,593 per cent., advances by 2,656 per cent., and their assets had increased
> by 905 per cent.[16]

In particular, the Society had a profound effect on home ownership in West Bromwich. Leslie Pearce was one of those who gained from his involvement with the Society. Then aged fifteen, he opened his first account in August 1925. It was for a quarter share, which was designed for juveniles and cost 7½d a week. The encouragement to apply came from Leslie's mother who 'promised to contribute 4½d (2p) on condition that I forfeited 3d from my then 6d (2½d) per week pocket money!' The deal was done 'but believe me, very difficult to endure in the days and weeks ahead'. When he started work Leslie made more savings from a very limited income, for at that time the average wage was £2 15s (£2.75) for a forty-eight hour week. By August 1933, he had a balance with the Society of £150, 'sufficient to qualify for a mortgage of £350, for the purchase of my first house at 59, Hope Street, West Bromwich, costing around £500'. Five years later, Leslie sold that house and moved to 15, Lily Street. Since then the West Bromwich has always been in the background of his life, 'playing its part whenever necessary'. Now retired, Leslie is 'moved to contemplate upon just how much of my comparative economic well-being may be considered due to my mother's encouragement and the WBBS's collaboration in 1925?'[17]

Emily Pardoe also became a member of the Society with a quarter share when she was fifteen – in her case in 1927. Living in West Bromwich she followed the example of both her mother and father who were already members. Emily continued to pay her dues after her marriage in 1937 and eventually she and her husband, James, opened a joint account. Unfortunately, two years later James was called up for service in the Royal Navy and 'I think owing to circumstance she had to draw out her savings whilst I was away'. Returning home in 1946, James, and Emily 'resumed our relationship with the Society and at that time we lived in West Bromwich'. By now James was working at the Bridge Foundry in West Bromwich. In 1951 he became a member of the firm's staff and made regular payments to the West Bromwich via his bank account, into which his wages were paid. Now aged eighty-five and eighty-seven respectively 'we are still members of your wonderful West Bromwich Building Society and have seen it grow and grow'.[18] Savers like James and Emily would have been familiar with the West Bromwich's home safes. Introduced during the inter-war years, these money boxes were kept by investors themselves and were used for saving coppers and silver. When they were full, they were brought to one of the Society's branches where they would be unlocked so that the money could be deposited in the saver's account.

By 1928 and excluding houses erected by the Corporation, 75% of the new dwellings in West Bromwich were purchased through the Society.[19] A year later it was noted that 'there were now 2,358 mortgages in force, which showed an average of one mortgage for every thirty-four inhabitants in West Bromwich – if all their business was with West Bromwich people, though obviously it was not'. A list of districts in which mortgaged properties were situated highlights this. It totalled 2,566, of which 1,275 – almost half – were in West Bromwich. After its own town, the Society was most represented in Birmingham, with 440 properties; Smethwick, with 186 properties; Oldbury and Langley, with 125 properties; and

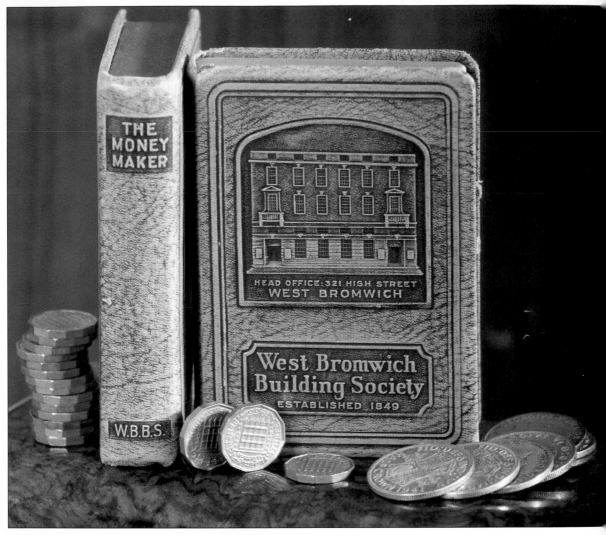

Saving through the decades – West Bromwich money boxes from a home safe to 1980s money boxes.

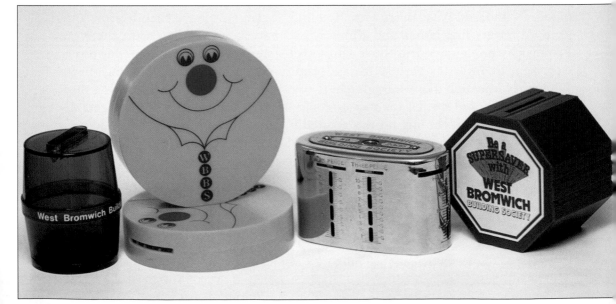

Tipton with 114 properties. Within Birmingham, Hall Green and Handsworth stood out with significant representation, whilst there were a noticeable number of mortgages in Warley and Quinton, Wednesbury and Darlaston, and Solihull, Shirley, Olton and Knowle. By contrast, the West Bromwich was weak in the west and south of the Black Country.[21]

The family of Mrs. Olive V. Patrick was amongst those outside the town who benefited from the Society. After the severe depression of the 1920s and early 1930s 'my parents were able to obtain a mortgage with the Society in 1932 in order to purchase a newly-built house in Walsall.' Olive used to travel to West Bromwich each month to make the repayments which 'I believe, amounted to £3 17s 6d'. Now aged eighty-one, she 'well remembers the enjoyment of a better home which my parents and the family had through having a mortgage with the West Bromwich'. Marrying in 1939 and moving to the south of England, she has recently invested with the Society 'for sentimental reasons'.[22]

With loans cheap and a need to reduce over-large reserves, building societies competed keenly for borrowers. Yet adhering to long-held principles, the West Bromwich was careful over its advances. From 1918 it had been prepared to lend up to 80% of certain freehold properties, but it was determined not to give mortgages recklessly.[23] In 1936 it refused loans to 11% of 'would-be borrowers' because it was not convinced either of the value or the quality of the property, and it enthusiastically adopted standard terms of business and a code of ethics and procedure drawn up by The National Association of Building Societies. This body had recently broken away from The Building Societies Association over the issue of the code, although four years later the two associations were re-united. The West Bromwich showed its commitment to the splinter group by introducing its scheme on 1 June 1936. That month the Society discontinued the twenty-five years mortgage term and replaced it by one of twenty-three years and five months.[24]

Firmly attached to the idea of playing fair and of not poaching 'on other people's preserves', the West Bromwich also maintained a firm commitment to the working class. Stress was laid upon the fact that the Society was mutual and that 'no one class' should profit above the other.[25] This adherence to its working-class roots was emphasised in 1937 by Alderman T. Cottrell, President of the West Bromwich. At a meeting of the Midland Federation of Building Societies, he asserted that there was 'still a desire on the part of the working classes in particular, to better themselves and become the possessors of their own houses'. There could be no more laudable an idea and it was the aim of the West Bromwich 'to see the working men of this country as well off, so to speak, as their "gaffers"'.[26] Yet there was a difficulty in achieving this aim. Large sums now had to be advanced to 'enable working people to acquire their own houses', whilst 'they had been compelled to advance money to speculative builders'.[27] That did not mean that the Society would 'encourage doubtful builders'. Indeed 'some of the present property being put forward at the present time was disgraceful'. Action needed to be taken by councils against such jerry builders for 'they were enriching themselves to the detriment of the poorer people'.[28]

Share certificate of Miss Winifred Mary Jessop, 24 January 1921.
(thanks to Miss Winifred Mary Jessop and Marie Baker of Stone Cross Branch Office)

Serious attempts were made to help working-class folk who wanted to buy their home. In the 1920s, 'through the good offices of a gentleman' who wished to be anonymous, 'the Society was able to advance, beyond their ordinary amount, the sum of £50 to bona-fide working men who found it difficult to provide the cash which represented the margin between the full purchase price and the Society's advance'. This £50 was loaned interest free from a trust fund of £1,000. When that was used up the philanthropic donor, Mr. K. A. Macaulay, gave another £500.[29] Then in 1932, it was reported that an approach had been received from an authority which was not nearby and which 'had decided to assist workmen in building houses'. The West Bromwich was asked to advance the mortgagors 90% of the valuation of the dwelling, provided that the council acted as guarantor. Normally the Society loaned up to 75% of the value and after consideration it was agreed to co-operate with the corporation, which would remain responsible for all loans until 'the amount is reduced to 66⅔% of the valuation'.

The authority was not named, although it was well known, and it was hoped that the Society's actions would 'enable the neighbouring Corporations to know that the Society was willing and able to come forward and help Municipalities in their desire to encourage people to own their own houses'.[30] Within a year, the West Bromwich had entered into an association with other local authorities, although now its advances were guaranteed by the councils until the loan had been reduced to 45% of the valuation of the property. Unfortunately 'they had not been able to obtain the guarantee of the West Bromwich Corporation' but it was hoped that this would happen so that mortgages could be advanced to 'many who otherwise might never be able to own a house of their own'.[31]

Front of Rule Book of West Bromwich Permanent Benefit Building Society, 1921.

1921.

WEST BROMWICH
Permanent Benefit Building Society,

301, HIGH STREET, WEST BROMWICH.

Established 1849.   Telephone 390.

President—
JOHN MARSTON, Esq.

Trustees—
ALDERMAN GEORGE GARRATT, J.P.
THOMAS WHITEHURST, Esq.
JOHN MARSTON, Esq.
ALDERMAN EDWARD ARNOLD.
COUNCILLOR THOMAS COTTRELL.

Solicitors—
MESSRS. WILLIAM BACHE & SONS, Lombard House.
MESSRS. L. & L. CLARK, 2, Lombard Street West,
MESSRS. CADDICK & WALKER, Lombard House,
all of West Bromwich.

Auditors—
CLEMENT KEYS, Esq., F.C.A., 71, Temple Row,
GEORGE T. COLEMAN, Esq., F.C.A., 13, Temple Street,
both of Birmingham.

Surveyor—
MR. JOHN W. ALLEN, 77, Bratt Street, West Bromwich.

Treasurer—
MR. THOMAS WHITEHURST.

Secretary—
MR. JOHN GARBETT.

Bankers—
LONDON JOINT CITY AND MIDLAND BANK, LTD.,
High Street, West Bromwich.

Woodhall & Son, Typs.

A New Head Office and Incorporation

As in the late nineteenth century, the growth of the West Bromwich ensured that it needed to increase its office space and in 1925 a building scheme was put forward. It was supported strongly by Clement Keys, one of the auditors. He stated that the present accommodation was restricted, whilst there was ample in the reserve fund to spend on new offices.[32] Two options were considered and dismissed: the re-building of the present offices, 'but that meant upper storeys

Advertisement for West Bromwich Permanent Benefit Building Society in Building Societies Year Book 1927.

The stone laying ceremony at the proposed new offices of West Bromwich Permanent Benefit Building Society at 321, High Street, 12 November 1926. Alderman Thomas Cottrell, vice-President of the Society, is holding the trowel, and fourth from his right is John Garbett, Secretary of the Society from 1905-36.

which did not commend itself to efficient working'; and the construction of new premises on land which had been sold recently to Kenrick and Jefferson, but that company would not enter into an agreement. This meant that a fresh site had to be purchased on the High Street and opposite the Town Hall.[33] A competition for the best plans was organised. It was assessed by W.A. Harvey, the consulting architect of the Bournville Village Trust, who was appointed by the Royal Institute. The winners were Surman and Benslyn, architects of Birmingham, who supervised the builders Elvin and Sons, also of Birmingham – and the stone-laying ceremony was carried out on 12 November 1926 by Councillor Tom Cottrell, Mayor of West Bromwich and vice-President of the Society.

The opening of the 'Home of Thrift', the new headquarters of West Bromwich Building Society at 321, High Street, 2 January 1928. Alderman Thomas Cottrell, President of West Bromwich Building Society, is standing on the left, behind the desk and below the clock. On his left is John Garbett, Secretary of the Society.

Costing about £30,000, the new offices were opened in January 1928 and were known as 'The Home of Thrift'.[34] Described as 'probably the most elaborately-equipped building in the town', it had a frontage of sixty-five feet, was faced in Portland stone, had balconies on the first floor and carved key-stones to the windows. Its 'dignified and striking' external appearance was matched by its interior, the main feature of which was 'a spacious banking hall, leading to which are two vestibules with marble floors and oak doors'. Interestingly the door of 'extraordinary quality' which secured the strong room was made by Messrs. Samuel Withers of West Bromwich – a firm established by relatives of the Samuel Withers who was one of the founders of the Society.[36]

The opening ceremony was attended by the Mayor of the town, Mrs. Cottrell, and 'a host of public people, not only of West Bromwich, but also of Wolverhampton, Walsall, Birmingham, Smethwick and Oldbury'. Congratulations were also sent on behalf of Wednesbury and Darlaston Councils and the Westminster Bank, which took over the Society's former headquarters. The opening itself was carried out by Councillor Cottrell, by then President of the Society. He pointed out that it was notable that 'while it took a period of 42 years to double the Society's assets, this had since been accomplished again in eight years – from 1919 to 1927'. Overall, since 1849 the West Bromwich had advanced £2,631,555 to enable people to own their homes – and 'of this sum over a million pounds had been advanced in the last 8½ years'. Assuming that the average advance had been £300 and that there were four persons to a house, 'the Society could claim to have found accommodation for over 35,000 people' – a figure over half the population of West Bromwich itself.[37]

The same year as the move to its new headquarters, the West Bromwich Permanent Benefit Building Society was incorporated under the Building Societies Act of 1874. At a special meeting, its name was changed to West Bromwich Building Society, new rules were adopted similar to those of all the larger societies, and the trustees were replaced by a board of directors.[38] The decision had been 'very carefully considered' and it was taken because incorporation would 'bring them into line with all the great Building Societies of the country whilst it would add to the simplification of the business'.[39] The ramifications of the change were explained by Frank Dilkes, later a distinguished managing director of the West Bromwich:

> we remained one of the oldest unincorporated Societies for a very long time. In an unincorporated Society there were Trustees of the funds and property and a Committee of Management, whilst when we were incorporated and became akin to a Company (or Corporation, as you would call it), we had a Board of Directors, and we were entitled to hold our own funds and property as a Corporate Body.[40]

A Changing Organisation

Following incorporation, Councillor Thomas Cottrell continued to act as President, having recently been elected following the death of Alderman Edward Arnold. A brewer operating from New Street, West Bromwich, Arnold himself had taken over in 1922 when John Marston had resigned due to ill health. Although not a councillor, Marston had been active in the community both as a church-warden and overseer of the poor. His 'sound advice and business acumen' were seen as playing 'no small part in fostering the progress and prosperity' of the West Bromwich.[41] Similar tributes were paid to Arnold when he died in 1922. Another former mayor, he had been a major figure in the town and in spite of a long illness he 'always endeavoured to do his duty'. One of those 'rare public men in England', he was characterised by his bluntness, straightforwardness, honesty and integrity. No-one could have surpassed him in his interest in the Society.[42]

From Little Acorns Grow

New Street, West Bromwich, about 1930. (with the permission of Sandwell Community History and Archives Service)

A works manager and later managing director born in West Bromwich, Cottrell had as his vice-President William Nock, another managing director. Both were amongst the last trustees. Their fellows included George Garratt, a provision merchant, who had held office since 1897; Frederick William Stamps, a brewer; and Reginald Alfred Siddons, an ironfounder belonging to the famous family of Hill Top manufacturers.[43] Only Garratt, aged eighty-six, did not move on to the new board of directors. Numbering eighteen men, they boasted six councillors – one of whom was the then mayor of West Bromwich and Bernard Smith who was later to become President and served the Society for more than sixty years. Except for Nock, who lived in Handsworth Wood, all of the directors had their homes within the borough. Of these, one director lived in Great Barr, another in Hill Top and the rest within West Bromwich town itself.

A mortgage passbook belonging to a Mr. Harold Sutton of Handsworth Wood. Mr. Sutton borrowed £400 in 1934, and cleared the mortgage ten years later making £8 a month repayments.

West Bromwich Building Society.

OFFICE HOURS.

Head Office—

321, HIGH STREET, WEST BROMWICH.

Monday	...	9-30 to 4 & 6 to 8
Tuesday	...	9-30 to 4
Wednesday	...	9-30 to 1
Thursday	...	9-30 to 4
Friday	...	9-30 to 4 & 6 to 8
Saturday	...	9-30 to 12

BRANCH OFFICES.

Handsworth— 205, Soho Road.
Open Daily.

Smethwick— 31, Cape Hill.
Open Daily.

Tipton— 32, Great Bridge.
Monday, 2 to 7-30.
Friday, 2 to 7-30.

Oldbury— 25, Birmingham Street.
Friday, 2 to 7-30.

No. 10248 Sig.

WEST BROMWICH BUILDING SOCIETY

ESTABLISHED 1849.

Incorporated under the Building Societies' Acts.

Head Office—
321, HIGH STREET, WEST BROMWICH.

Telephone—West Bromwich 0390.

JOHN GARBETT,
Secretary.

This loyalty to the borough was reflected in the professionals who served the Society: the surveyor, Herbert Arnold, was based at 321 High Street; both the solicitors, William Bache and Sons and J. and L. Clark, had their main offices in the town; and one of the auditors, Clement Keys, was also in the High Street. The exception was the other auditor, George Coleman, who worked from Bennetts Hill, Birmingham.[44] From 1933, the auditors were appointed not as individuals but as firms, 'although the audit would be done by the same people in the same excellent way'.[45] Both men were long-standing in their commitment to the West Bromwich. Clement Keys himself was presented with a silver tankard in 1936 to recognise his fiftieth annual audit, whilst George Coleman's father had been one of the founders of the Society.[46] He had told his son that 'on contribution nights a body-guard of Committee-men used to take the Treasurer home, the money being in a black leather bag'. He also recounted that when the book-keeping became too much to be done by a clerk in a solicitor's office then someone was approached to carry out the duties. He was diffident 'and so one of the members of the Committee went to him and said that if he would fulfil the duties, he would give him a hundred pounds – and no-one would be the wiser'. The secret was kept until 1933 when it was revealed that the benefactor was R.S. Hudson, a trustee and businessman who invented the famous Hudson's Dry Soap used in washing clothes.[47]

The directors were actively involved in the work of six sub-committees, like that which oversaw the running of the office, and from 1934 received a remuneration for their services.[48] Still, one of the most important figures in the Society was its secretary, John Garbett. Appointed in 1905, he held his post for thirty years until he was elected a director and co-opted on to the General Purposes Committee.[49] Garbett was instrumental in drawing up the new rules needed because of incorporation and oversaw the Society's expansion outside West Bromwich. In particular he was valued because he 'was introducing capable men into the atmosphere of building society work'. Each junior was trained for responsible positions and staff received tuition towards exams from The Building Societies Institute. It was also during Garbett's tenure that a staff superannuation contributory fund was set up in 1930, coming into operation four years later. The first chairman of The Building Societies' Secretaries Association, he was one of the original members of the West Bromwich Cinderella Club, later superseded by the Poor Children's Welfare Society.[50] John Garbett's successor as secretary was his assistant of twelve years, John Scott Wright.

A qualified chartered accountant, he had joined the Society in 1922 and soon became respected for his professionalism, knowledge and integrity. Straightforward in his manner, he was a successful devisor of methods of operation and had the complete confidence of the board of the West Bromwich.

Obviously, incorporation meant that the West Bromwich had to change in its organisation and some of its practices. Yet it did not lead to a change in approach. As Councillor Cottrell emphasised, it continued to appeal to the smaller investors and borrowers 'and those are the people we want to help, rather than have the

John Scott Wright, behind his desk at the 'Home of Thrift'. He was appointed assistant secretary of West Bromwich Permanent Benefit Building Society in 1924, became Secretary in 1936 and two years later was made Manager of the Society, 1938.

rich associated with the Society. I always looked upon this Society as the poor man's salvation – and I am more than ever satisfied that this is the truth of the position'. In a move to ensure that the Society reached out more effectively to working-class people, expansion was sought outside West Bromwich.[51] As early as 1871, a suggestion had been made that an agency should be opened at Cannock or Birmingham to facilitate the making of advances.[52]

Nothing came of that proposal, but in 1928 the Society opened branches at 84, Waterloo Road, Smethwick, 25, Birmingham Street, Oldbury and 32, Great Bridge, Tipton. It was believed that these offices 'would tend to educate the people of those towns to something of the degree they had educated the people of West Bromwich in the matter of thrift and self-help'. This development came after Cottrell had been approached by the authorities of the Birmingham Municipal Bank to enquire whether 'he would have any objection to a branch of that institution being established in West Bromwich'. The reply was unequivocal – the Society 'was doing the job with equal satisfaction'.[53]

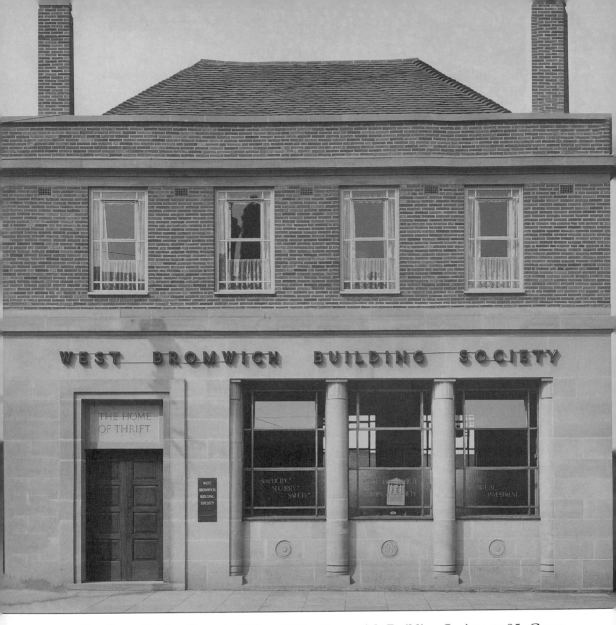

The Great Bridge Branch Office of West Bromwich Building Society at 85, Great Bridge, opened 3 June 1935 and replacing the original branch opened in June 1928.

Office hours at the Home of Thrift were 9.30 a.m. to 4.00 p.m. each day, except on Wednesdays when closing was at 1.00 p.m. and on Saturday when it was 12.00 noon. Mondays and Tuesdays the headquarters was also open from 6.00 p.m. until 8.00 p.m. At the Smethwick branch, staff served customers on Mondays and Fridays from 2.00 p.m. until 7.30 p.m. The Oldbury branch was open for the same hours on a Friday, with the Great Bridge branch opening only on a Monday. By now and as they had done since 1849, members were still paying 5s a fortnight for £120 investing shares which participated in profits – usually at the rate of 5% annually.[54] Fines continued to be levied on defaulting members, at the rate for each share of a penny a month or part thereof.[55]

Additionally there were £10 investing shares, payable at 2s or more each month, which gained an annual fixed interest of 4¼% but did not benefit from profits; and £10 paid up shares with a fixed interest of 4%. These were issued in any number up to ten, were free of tax, were non-participating in profits and allowed withdrawals at short notice. Finally there were £10 shares savings certificates, free of tax, which gained interest over ten years, and deposits of £1 upwards. Again these were tax exempt and received an interest of 3½% a year. To encourage further saving, home safes were issued free, provided a new account was opened with at least an initial deposit of 2s 6d.[56]

All three new branches made a profit in their first year and in 1931 the West Bromwich opened another branch in Handsworth. This had been deemed

*The Handsworth Branch Office of West Bromwich Building Society
at 205, Soho Road, Handsworth, opened 4 May 1931.*

necessary as 'it had to be realised that there were other building societies coming to Birmingham and nearer and nearer to West Bromwich'.[57] This statement alluded to the increasing competition amongst building societies which was leading some bodies to expand outside their 'natural sphere of influence'. In a further move to reinforce its position locally the next year the West Bromwich took over new premises at 31, Cape Hill. The move from Waterloo Road was necessitated because of 'the large connection at Smethwick' which had seen the Society advance in twelve months upwards of £38,000 'upon the security of leasehold and freehold property in Smethwick, Warley and Quinton'. Previously the Cape Hill Post Office, the building was altered considerably by G. and H. Marshall of Smethwick according to plans drawn by Arnold and Hewitt of West Bromwich. In keeping with the Home of Thrift and other branches, the Cape Hill offices had a 'neo-Graeco' feeling and 'is carried out in Portland Stone and sand-faced bricks, with bronze semi-circular head windows and grilles'. A banking hall, manager's office and strong room occupied most of the ground floor, whilst above was a suite of offices. As at the head office, some of these rooms were let. The counter was constructed of oak with bronze grilles and fittings, and the same wood was used for the wall panelling, doors and stationery cupboard, whilst the frieze and ceiling was decorated by fibrous plaster. Mr. J.G. Hall A.C.A. was appointed manager and he and his staff opened the office each day and also on Monday and Friday evenings.[58]

New premises soon followed in prominent positions at both Oldbury and Great Bridge.[59] The importance of these branches was made clear by Phyllis W. Adams. With a sum of £10, she was one of those who opened an account at Great Bridge in 1937. Gripping 'my own book, I felt like a princess'. Thirteen years previously her mother had no option but to travel to West Bromwich to pay her money into her account. Phyllis used 'to be bored and fidgety waiting for ages, in a queue in a long dark room with a lighted office at the far end'.[60]

Similar memories are held by Maggie Bryan (then Barker) now aged ninety-five. Before the First World War she had a quarter share in the West Bromwich, as did her mother and sister. Each of them paid 7½d a week and every fortnight they came on the tram from Toll End, Tipton to settle up their dues in West Bromwich. They went to a hall inside which was a high table, 'behind which a row of men were sitting on stools'. People queued around the room and when the woman's turn came 'she handed over her pass book and 1s 3d – being two weeks' money'. The first man shouted out the number of her share and the amount. Then he passed her book to the next man, who repeated the procedure and put the amount into both his ledger and her book. This was passed along to the end and returned to her, whilst the money was put into a big cash box. The chief man involved was James Withers, who served as check steward for many years until his resignation in 1920.[61] His duties in checking the number and initials of each member and the amount they were to pay in corresponded to Maggie Bryan's recollections, as did the job of the cash steward who actually received the money.[62]

The 'Home of Thrift', the headquarters of West Bromwich Building Society at 321, High Street.

Following incorporation, the roles of check and cash stewards disappeared. The West Bromwich was set upon becoming a modern and progressive society with a trained staff, purpose-built headquarters and new branches. Yet for all it looked forward, it remained deeply attached to the values of its founders, and it did not eschew its adherence to fair dealing, integrity, mutuality and support for the working class. Well-organised and well-managed, by 1938, the West Bromwich was in a strong position. It had extended beyond its original confines, its assets had reached over £3 million, and its membership was approaching 30,000.[63] A year later for the first time in its history, its receipts exceeded £2 million, but any hopes of sustained growth were dashed as war once more ravaged Europe.[64]

Chapter 4:

Building the Society, 1939-78

The Effects of The Second World War

At the outbreak of the war, the building society movement appeared to be triumphantly leading the way to a nation dominated by owner-occupiers. Since the end of the Great War its shareholders had grown by over 300% to more than two million; its borrowers had expanded by the same proportion to one and half million; and its total assets had expanded spectacularly from £68 million to £773 million. Overall, throughout the inter-war years 2.9 million private houses had been built compared with 1.1 million council houses.[1] Many of these homes had been erected in the five years from 1933. In the opinion of Harold Bellman, Chairman of The National Association of Building Societies, this building boom was made a reality only because of the movement he headed.[2] The massive expansion in house ownership affected mostly the middle class but it did have a wider significance in that it helped to drag Great Britain out of the Depression. This was achieved through creating a demand not only for building materials and workers, but also for household goods, furnishings and road works.

For all the strengths of the building society movement, it faced problems because of an intense competition for mortgages. This led most societies to extend their terms of repayment from between sixteen and twenty years to between twenty-one and twenty-five years; and it encouraged them to develop schemes to lend more than was customary. Societies tended to advance no more than 70-75% of the value of a house, but there were two main ways to increase this amount. First, through insurance company guarantees covering the amount in excess of what the Society would usually lend. This was achieved via a single premium paid by the borrower to the insurance company, which was then able to compensate the Society if there were losses. It was a popular move and continued as the Building Societies Indemnity Scheme. There is no suggestion that the West Bromwich adopted the scheme, although it did make arrangements 'with a leading life assurance company whereby on a slightly increased repayment, a borrower may take out a temporary reducing life policy, so that in the event of death during the period of the mortgage, the balance outstanding will be wiped off and the deeds handed over to the deceased borrower's representative.'[3]

A second way whereby societies could lend more than was usual was achieved by involvement with builders' pools. Builders who were keen to sell their dwellings often needed purchasers who could raise 85% to 90% of the value. In these

Staff of West Bromwich Building Society, 1940. John Scott Wright, Manager and Secretary of the Society is seated in the middle of the front row. On his right is William Lloyd Williams, assistant secretary.

circumstances certain builders deposited the difference between the two sums with a building society – this amount serving as a guarantee if a borrower or borrowers defaulted. Again there is no evidence of the West Bromwich becoming involved in such a practice and given its abhorrence of jerry builders it would appear unlikely that pool business was acceptable to the Society. Similarly, although the West Bromwich acted to protect its local interest by opening branches it did not seek to 'poach' on the territory of others – as did a number of large and leading societies.

The high principles of the West Bromwich appeared to be validated by the government in 1939 when it passed another Building Societies Act. This legislation arose from a well-publicised legal battle between Mrs. Elsey Borders and the Bradford Third Equitable Building Society which was involved with builders' pools. The plaintiff claimed that the house that she had purchased was built badly and had been advertised in an overly favourable manner by the builder. Moreover she averred that the Society was aware of this fact when it loaned her the money for a mortgage. The case was not settled until 1941 but it attracted the notice of government which decided to act to give security to building society members. Amongst other matters, the new law fixed the advance to a member upon the security of freehold or leasehold property. As a result a society no longer had the power to take into account the value of any additional security taken by the society except in specified cases – such as charges upon life assurance policies and guarantees by local authorities. From now on building

Warrant for interest on £10 paid up shares in
West Bromwich Building Society, 30 September 1941.

WEST BROMWICH BUILDING SOCIETY

ESTABLISHED 1849 - - - - - - TELEPHONE WEST BROMWICH 0741

HEAD OFFICE - - - - - 321 HIGH STREET, WEST BROMWICH

30th September, 1941

Dear Sir or Madam,

I have pleasure in attaching warrant for Interest on your £10 Paid-up Shares with this Society for the half-year ending 30th September, 1941.

Kindly complete the form of receipt at foot and cash within 10 days.

I shall be glad if you will inform me immediately of any change of address so that all communications may reach you promptly.

NOTE—
By arrangement with the Commissioners of Inland Revenue the Society is directly assessed in respect of the liability of its Investors to Income Tax at the standard rate on dividends or interest from the Society. No Income Tax at the standard rate is repayable to or chargeable upon Investors in respect of such income, but Investors are required to include the income in their return of total income for Income Tax and Sur-Tax purposes.

Yours obediently,
JOHN SCOTT WRIGHT,
Manager and Secretary

TEAR OFF HERE

societies were 'more careful to put in a disclaimer that the mortgage granted implied a particular market value for the property concerned'.[4]

This Act was passed in September 1939, the same month in which the United Kingdom was drawn into the Second World War. As in the Great War, house building all but stopped, and the income of building societies dropped because they drastically reduced their advances on new properties. Such a profound difficulty was compounded by a marked decline in the amount saved with building societies, caused by the movement of funds into government savings schemes designed to aid the war effort. Some societies had a £50 annual limit for new investments. In the case of the West Bromwich, its receipts 'shrank enormously, if not alarmingly; the slope from the heights of the 1939 figures to a level approaching that of the slump years of the 1930s was traversed in three short years – from £2,266,478 at the outbreak of the war to £638,686 in the dark days of 1942'.[5]

With a falling income and drops in both its advances and savings accounts, the West Bromwich Building Society also had to cope with high demands on its funds made by the government. In particular, and like all societies, it was affected by an increase in the income tax which it paid. The importance of this levy was made plain by Alderman Thomas Cottrell in May 1942 at the Annual General Meeting of the Society. He declared that 'we don't begrudge it. In fact we are glad to be able to pay it'. To make provision for the increase in income tax, the Society had lowered its interest rates to investors, without which 'the whole thing would be hopeless'. Still, it was worth bearing in mind that 'the Society pays the tax and what the investors get is tax-free'.[6]

In addition to the raised income tax and again in common with other societies, the West Bromwich also had to make payments to the National Defence Contribution and the War Damage Contribution. This last fund was available for repairs to property affected by enemy action. Unfortunately, there were many such premises in the West Midlands. Because of its industrial importance to the war effort, the region was a major target for the Nazis and bombs on High Street, West Bromwich hit the home of former secretary John Garbett, as well as the offices of the Society's solicitors, William Bache and Sons.[7]

Ruby Greathead was also affected badly by bombing. She had opened her first account with the West Bromwich in 1927 when she was sixteen. Like her father, Ernest Wale, she was employed in the Post Office and from her 13s a week wage she would always put a small amount in the Society. During the Blitz on the West Midlands she lived in Great Barr and when an explosive fell nearby in Newton Road it smashed a water main which ran close to her house. The flow of water caused one wall of her home to subside. Ruby applied to the relevant authorities for assistance, but her request was turned down for technical reasons. In desperation she turned to the West Bromwich: 'The house kept sinking. The manager at the Great Barr Branch was very kind. He took me on trust and loaned me around £1,000 to repair the damage caused by the German bomb. I paid it back as soon as I possibly could.' Now aged eighty-eight, Ruby stays loyal to the Society and regularly visits the branch in Shrewsbury, where she now lives.[8]

John E. McDonald was on the staff of the West Bromwich during this time. Joining the Society in 1937, he worked on the counter and also as one of only two outside representatives. One of his areas was Coventry and his daughter, Joan recalls:

I can remember him telling me about the time when Coventry was bombed. He set out as usual but was not allowed into the city, the cathedral was destroyed and it was several days before he was able to get into Coventry. The devastation made a great impression on him. He also told me about the day when the buildings opposite the Head Office were bombed – next to the Public Library. From the upstairs window you could see right across to the District Hospital – now Edward Street Hospital. He and his colleagues took their turn fire watching – from the Building Society roof, I believe.

Letter from The Building Societies Institute advising John McDonald of his election as an Associate of the Institute, 3 March 1949. (thanks to Joan McDonald)

THE BUILDING SOCIETIES INSTITUTE

E. C. L. BUTLER
SECRETARY

MAYFAIR 0515

14, PARK STREET.

LONDON. W.1.

7th march, 1949.

Dear Sir,

ASSOCIATESHIP

I have much pleasure in informing you that, at the last meeting of the Council, you were duly elected an Associate of the Institute.

I have pleasure in enclosing a copy of the Report of the Council 1948-1949 and the list of Publications. The Constitution and Bye-Laws and the Syllabus of Examinations will shortly be reprinted to incorporate current amendments and a copy of each will be sent to you in due course. If however, you require one immediately I will send you one on request.

The Institute publishes a journal entitled "B.S.I. Quarterly". A copy of the current issue,(if available) is enclosed, and future copies will be sent to you as they are published.

The Institute mainatins a comprehensive lending Library at its headquarters and books may be borrowed by post. A copy of the Library Catalogue will be sent to you on request.

The annual subscription of Associates is £1. 11. 6d due on 1st January in each year, and the proportion of your subscription now due for the period 1st April to 31st December, 1949 is £1. 3. 6d. Remittances should be made payable to "The Building Societies Institute", and should be crossed and sent to me at this address.

Yours faithfully,

Secretary.

P.S. I also enclose the Agenda for the Annual General meeting.

J.E. McDonald, Esq., A.B.S.

A 30ft advertising hoarding in Navigation Street, Birmingham, in 1948. This site cost the Society £20 a year.

When Joan was about sixteen and because the family had no telephone she had to go and tell Mr. John Scott Wright, the manager and secretary, that her father was ill with flu. She went to the counter and was then shown into Mr. Scott Wright's office on the ground floor. Joan found the experience quite intimidating as the manager sat behind his great desk – although 'he was actually very kind'. In the years immediately following the war Miss Phyllis Jones was in charge of the typists, and 'she was very kind to me as a child'; whilst all the staff would go on outings to places like Stratford and have 'a punt on the river'.[9]

The financial affairs of the West Bromwich improved slightly in 1943, and by 1944, its receipts had reached only £675,906.[10] Despite these low levels of income, the West Bromwich emerged from the war with large surplus funds simply because it had not been able to lend much. It recognised the plight of many hard-up borrowers who had fought in the war and offered to extend the terms of the mortgage for all war servicemen by at least another five years.

Its position was similar to that of every other society, as was its ability to fund mortgages in peacetime. At first that potential was not realised. The Labour government of 1945 was determined to back with subsidies a massive programme of council house building. At the same time private building was restricted by the continuation of the wartime policy of licensing new construction. In this situation, most building society activity related to mortgages advanced on existing properties.

Centenary celebrations of West Bromwich Building Society, Saturday 23 April 1949. Left to right: John Scott Wright, Manager and Secretary; Alderman George C. W. Jones, Mayor of West Bromwich; Frederick William Stamps, President of the Society; Sir Charles Davies J.P., Chairman of the Council of The Building Societies Association; Reginald Alfred Sissons, vice-President of the Society; and John Dugdale, M.P., Financial Secretary to the Admiralty and MP for West Bromwich.

Perversely, matters for societies improved slightly after the economic crisis of 1947. This led the government to cut back on all of its social programmes, including that of council house building. In the same year, an effort was made 'to close the tax loopholes whereby big money investors get exemption under the tax-free dividend system'. In effect, the system was not tax free but it was a 'special rate of income tax, only 37% of the standard rate, paid on interest and distributed profits by the building societies'.[11]

The Post-War Expansion in Home Ownership

The three years from 1947 saw a pronounced upturn in the fortunes of building societies. By 1949, its centenary year, the West Bromwich itself had attained a gross income of £2,240,870, advanced £1,590,241 and achieved total assets of £5,059,245.[12] This position was bettered markedly the next year during which the Society's assets rose to more than £6 million. Overall there were now 1.56 million

The cover of the Society's Centenary Celebration Booklet 1949.

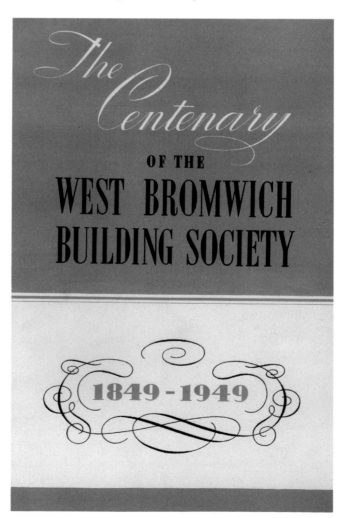

depositors and shareholders in the nation's building societies, six million more than in 1949. Frederick William Stamps, president of the West Bromwich, felt that this increase 'was a clear indication that the faith the public had in building societies was not diminishing'. Moreover if controls were relaxed to a greater extent 'many more would avail themselves of the services of building societies'.[13]

Stamps had been appointed in 1946, following the death of Alderman Thomas Cottrell. Born, bred and educated in West Bromwich, he had been managing director of Samuel Woodall's Brewery until 1938 when it was taken over by Hanson's of Dudley. Intimately associated with Mayers Green Congregational Church, his connection with the West Bromwich had begun eighteen years previously when he had been elected to the Committee of Management. In 1927, he became a trustee and a year later with the Society's incorporation he was made a life director. Stamps was supported in his role by his vice-President, Reginald A. Siddons. Chairman of J. and J. Siddons of Hill Top, he had 'an unbroken association of thirty-two years with the Building Society, having first been elected to the Committee of Management in 1913'.[14] In keeping with his longstanding commitment to the Society, Siddons was a firm believer in carrying out properly the two main functions of the West Bromwich: 'to provide safe and lucrative investments for the thrifty, and to provide the wherewithal for those who had found them'.[15]

Advertisement for West Bromwich Building Society in Building Societies Year Book 1949.

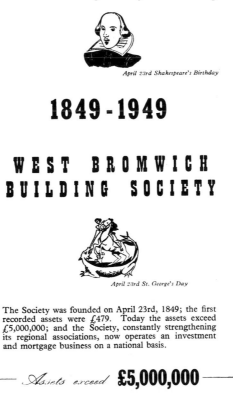

April 23rd Shakespeare's Birthday

1849 - 1949

WEST BROMWICH BUILDING SOCIETY

April 23rd St. George's Day

The Society was founded on April 23rd, 1849; the first recorded assets were £479. Today the assets exceed £5,000,000; and the Society, constantly strengthening its regional associations, now operates an investment and mortgage business on a national basis.

—— *Assets exceed* **£5,000,000** ——

West Bromwich Building Society, Head Office—West Bromwich. Manager and Secretary: John Scott Wright, A.C.A., F.B.S.

The relaxation of building controls sought by the West Bromwich and other building societies came swiftly after the election of a Conservative government late in 1951. Private construction was 'effectively unfettered' and although many council houses were built in the early years of the Conservative's term in office, 'policy swung firmly behind the expansion of owner-occupation'.[16] The shift towards private building was boosted by a number of concrete measures: in 1953 the cost of new construction under the Town and Country Planning Act of 1947 was reduced by the abolition of development charges; for three years from 1954 excess advances were guaranteed by the government; from 1957 the decontrol of rents in the private sector meant that many mortgage repayments became cheaper than many rents; and from 1958 there was a reduction in stamp duty for houses priced below £3,000. The government also actively supported building societies by lending them £100 million over the three years from 1959 to encourage advances on houses built before 1919. Finally, in 1962 owner-occupiers were exempted from income tax under Schedule 'A'.

Government backing went hand-in-hand with social change. Income levels were going up for upper working-class folk and this phenomenon combined with rising expectations and a desire for material improvement ensured that there would be plenty of people seeking mortgages. This demand remained high despite the substantial post-war increase in house prices. Unsurprisingly, this had been most pronounced in the late 1940s when the slow pace of rebuilding could not match the need for private homes. This meant that in the heartland of the West Bromwich, it cost £2,000 to buy a three-bedroomed semi-detached house. By comparison a similar property had cost £450 ten years earlier. House prices continued to rise even after private house construction gathered pace in the 1950s – with the result that by the end of that decade the same kind of house was fetching £2,750.

The more favoured circumstances for building societies did not mean that they were not faced with problems. Overall, financial institutions of all kinds were affected by a credit squeeze, whilst stiff competition for savers was provided by tax-free interest concessions allowed by the government to the Post Office and Trustee Savings Banks. Still, the period from 1951 saw 'building societies make very rapid, if uneven, progress' and advances by building societies rose sharply to £373 million in 1954. After this there was a four-year period of stability, followed by another marked increase to £517 million in 1959 – after which there was a gradual climb to £612 million in 1962. Then in the ensuing year advances rose dramatically to £849 million. These spectacular figures were not necessarily matched in the number of properties the purchase of which was financed by building societies. Because of the increase in house prices, advances went forward more slowly – albeit significantly. In 1951 there had been 302,000 and by 1963 there were 477,000.[17]

According to the *Building Societies Year Book* of 1955/56, the West Bromwich recorded 'a phenomenal increase in business' in these years. Its assets now exceeded £9.5 million, its reserves amounted to £425,000 and its annual receipts were more than £3.25 million. On these figures, the assets of the West Bromwich

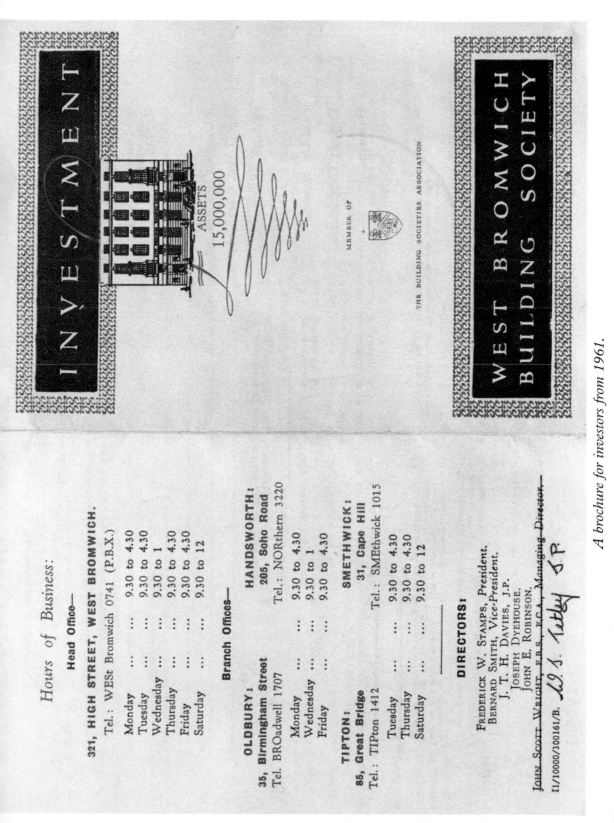

INVESTMENT

WEST BROMWICH BUILDING SOCIETY

ASSETS
15,000,000

MEMBER OF

THE BUILDING SOCIETIES ASSOCIATION

Hours of Business

Head Office

321, HIGH STREET, WEST BROMWICH.

Tel.: WESt Bromwich 0741 (P.B.X.)

Monday	...	9.30 to 4.30
Tuesday	...	9.30 to 4.30
Wednesday	...	9.30 to 1
Thursday	...	9.30 to 4.30
Friday	...	9.30 to 4.30
Saturday	...	9.30 to 12

Branch Offices

OLDBURY:
35, Birmingham Street
Tel. BROadwell 1707

Monday	...	9.30 to 4.30
Wednesday	...	9.30 to 1
Friday	...	9.30 to 4.30

HANDSWORTH:
205, Soho Road
Tel.: NORthern 3220

TIPTON:
85, Great Bridge
Tel.: TIPton 1412

Tuesday	...	9.30 to 4.30
Thursday	...	9.30 to 4.30
Saturday	...	9.30 to 12

SMETHWICK:
31, Cape Hill
Tel.: SMEthwick 1015

DIRECTORS:

FREDERICK W. STAMPS, *President.*
BERNARD SMITH, *Vice-President.*
J. T. H. DAVIES, J.P.
JOSEPH DYEHOUSE.
JOHN E. ROBINSON.
JOHN SCOTT WRIGHT, F.B.S., F.C.A., *Managing Director.*

11/10000/300161/B.

A brochure for investors from 1961.

Above: The main banking hall at the 'Home of Thrift', the headquarters of West Bromwich Building Society, late 1960s.

Below: The general office at the 'Home of Thrift', the headquarters of West Bromwich Building Society, late 1960s.

*A 1950s weekend school for building society staff including representatives from
West Bromwich Building Society. (thanks to Joan McDonald)*

were over twice those of the Wolverhampton and District Permanent Building
Society; almost twice as much as those of the Wolverhampton Freeholders'
Permanent Building Society; three times as great as those of the South
Staffordshire Building Society; and at least seven times as much respectively as
the Wednesbury Building Society, the Tipton and Coseley Permanent Building
Society; and the Walsall Mutual Building Society. Clearly the leading building
society in the Black Country, in the wider Midlands, the West Bromwich was
exceeded by the Coventry Permanent Economic Society with assets of more than
£14 million; the Leek and Moorlands Building Society with assets of £29 million;
and the Leicester Permanent Building Society with assets of £31 million. These
last two societies were at the top of the middle league of building societies
nationally, overshadowed still by the likes of the Halifax Building Society which
had assets of £214 million.[18]

From Little Acorns Grow

Perhaps influenced by its waxing affairs as much as by its distinguished history, the West Bromwich sought letters patent from the College of Arms for the grant of armorial bearings. Approved in 1955, the arms were designed by Mr. H. Ellis Tomlinson M.A. of Lancashire, the heraldic adviser to The Building Societies

The Armorial Bearings of West Bromwich Building Society, granted 22 July 1955.

Association. He placed a white stag's head on a blue shield. These features were taken from the arms of West Bromwich Borough, and symbolised the close associations between the corporation and the Society. Topping the stag's head, a Stafford Knot represented the county to which the Society belonged and in which it had its principal sphere of influence. Across the top of the shield an embattled line suggested the idea of the Englishman's home as his castle, whilst the black portion which surmounted it represented the industrial background of the Black Country. Against this scene, home ownership, thrift and security were indicated by gold keys and a sprig of thrift. Above the shield was placed a closed helm 'proper to civic and other corporate arms'. Upon the helm, the dragon and pennon of St George and the lance from Shakespeare's arms represented the foundation of the West Bromwich on 23 April. All three rose from a celestial crown of stars which indicated the Methodist School Rooms in Paradise Street. The arms were completed by the motto 'Sapientia Aedificatur Domus' – 'Through wisdom is a house built'.[19]

The continued growth of building societies in general led to further legislation. From 1959, and subject to conditions laid down by the Chief Registrar, societies were allowed to accept the investments of trustees without special authorisation under the trust deed. The next year another Building Societies Act entailed that liquid funds should be just that and be safe. It also gave more powers to the Chief Registrar and restricted the size of loans. Then in 1962 one more

Staff photo, January 1956.

Act consolidated all previous legislation that affected building societies. Such legislation was in no way intended to restrict the activities of building societies and in particular, the West Bromwich maintained its impressive growth. By 1963, when its President Frederick Stamps died, the Society's assets had risen to £18 million.[20]

His successor was Bernard Smith, principal partner in Wm Bache and Sons, the solicitors of the West Bromwich for many years. Interestingly, Clement Keys and Son still remained the Society's auditors. Under the chairmanship of Bernard Smith, growth accelerated throughout the 1960s and 1970s. As with all building societies, the expansion of the West Bromwich was aided by the widespread desire for home ownership, which meant that the number of privately-owned houses continued to rise dramatically. Second, it was assisted by a shift in the policy of the Labour Party, whereby it came to adhere to the ideal of a property-owning democracy and continued to support owner-occupiers after it came to office in 1964. In particular it sought ways to extend the phenomenon from the upper working class to the middle and poorer working class.

This motive was the impetus to the Option and Mortgage Guarantee Scheme of 1967 which was 'specifically designed to reduce the mortgage rate for the lower-income workers'. The measure sought to achieve its aim by introducing subsidies which were equivalent to tax relief for those borrowers whose incomes were too low to pay income tax. Additionally it guaranteed loans up to the full value of the purchase house and so lowered the need to search for a deposit. A third factor aiding building societies was the decision of the Conservative government of 1974 to focus on first-time buyers. Not only did it loan building societies money to keep the mortgage rate below 9½% but also it offered certain house-buyers interest-free loans and a tax-free bonus.[21]

During the 1970s banks did not see mortgage provision as their role and restricted business to current accounts, personal loans and corporate finance. Also the building society movement continued to operate as a cartel through The Building Societies Association whereby each society agreed to charge the same lending and savings rates.

Expanding the West Bromwich Building Society

As in the 1950s, the development in home ownership during the 1960s was achieved despite harsh economic conditions. A continued credit squeeze meant that there was a shortfall in the amount of money available to lenders. In turn this led to the introduction of quotas, such as the insistence that a mortgage would be granted by the West Bromwich only to those folk who had been saving in an account for at least six months. Yet it was not easy to draw in investors. Bank base rates rose to 7%, ensuring that such institutions could pay more attractive rates than could building societies. Still, the thirst for home ownership remained undiminished and this factor alone meant that building societies maintained their growth.

The West Bromwich was in the forefront of the expansion of the building society movement. Its higher profile was the result not only of external factors but also of an internal initiative – the decision 'to build the Society'. This was greatly the responsibility of Frank Dilkes. Formerly with the Nottingham Building Society, he had moved on to become Assistant Secretary at the Dewsbury and West Riding Building Society. Deeply experienced and with professional qualifications as a Bachelor of Laws and a Chartered Secretary, he was to have a major

Frank Dilkes pictured in 1957, a year before he joined the Society.

Frank Dilkes at his desk in the new purpose-built Principal Office.

influence on the progress of the West Bromwich. He became its assistant manager in 1958 and three years later was promoted to general manager. Then in 1961 Frank Dilkes became general manager following the death of Mr. John Scott Wright, the Managing Director. The bond between the Society and its staff was emphasised by a provision in Mr. Scott Wright's will. With no immediate family he left the residue of his estate to be shared between the Society's Directors and full-time staff. The amount given to each individual depended upon their length of service and remuneration. John Scott Wright himself was remembered by The Council of the Building Societies Institute – upon which he had served for many years. The Society set up and awarded the John Scott Wright Memorial Prize which was judged by the Institute for the best paper of sufficient merit each year in the subject of building society administration.

The victorious Albion F.A. Cup side display their trophy in High Street, outside the Society's office, 1968.

Jean George, Tony Hannigan and Diane Flint collecting toys for a Childrens' Christmas Charity at the Walsall branch in 1974.

With imagination, foresight and ability Frank Dilkes took charge of policy and development. From 1965 his position was strengthened when he was elected to the board of the Society and became its managing director. Importantly he forged a vital partnership with Leslie Tinkler, Assistant General Manager, another experienced and knowledgeable building society professional who had been assistant secretary at the Walsall Mutual Society. At the West Bromwich, Leslie Tinkler took over most of the responsibilities for administration and managing of mortgages and mortgage quotas. He was elected to the board in 1971 and became deputy managing director.[22]

Well known across the industry Frank Dilkes sat on a number of trade bodies and held a range of senior positions. These included 25 years as a member of The Chartered Building Societies Institute, of which he was National President in 1972/73; he served twenty-two years on the Committee of The Midland Association of Building Societies and was both President and Chairman. Regionally, he served on the Sandwell Association of Industry and Commerce and The Council of the Birmingham Chamber of Commerce and Industry.

Frank Dilkes's policy of 'building the Society' had four main features: the development of a modern system of administration and accounting; the move to a large, purpose-built headquarters; the opening of full branches; and 'the eternal struggle to maintain the percentage of Reserves to growth in Assets'.[23] The preservation of a large reserve ratio was achieved through making surpluses from current activities and keeping management expenses low. This lack of reduction in the reserves meant that the West Bromwich could expand without risk and do so 'scientifically'. Growth itself took place through 'obtaining investment money by opening branches in new areas'. As Leslie Tinkler explained, some market research was done before a branch was opened 'on the basis of footfall, and the success of a branch helped to generate further branches'.[24]

Expansion began in 1965. Frank Dilkes had persuaded the board that the Society could achieve little further expansion without the opening of full branch offices, emphasising that if this was not done then assets would be lost to other societies. His recommendation was accepted and it was decided to open branches in places where there was little or no building society activity. As a first step in the policy of expansion the four sub-offices in Handsworth, Great Bridge, Oldbury and Smethwick were refurbished and opened full-time. A year later in 1965, new branches were opened in Great Barr, Leicester and Coventry. Within three years, the West Bromwich had enhanced its powerful position in its West Midlands hinterland by the setting up of other branches in Stone Cross, Walsall, Kingswinford, Wolverhampton and at Hall Green and Temple Street, Birmingham.

At the same time a strong thrust had been outwards through new branches in Chester and Manchester. These branches were supplemented by collecting agencies in places like Wrexham, Norwich, Sunderland and Blackpool.[25] Frank Dilkes ensured that the 'active policy of Branch development' was pushed forward and by 1971 the West Bromwich boasted twenty-three offices, whilst another

Principal Office under construction, 1976.

The new Principal Office takes shape.

fourteen were planned to open that year. One of them was the branch in Welshpool. Built by Deacon and Boardman of Walsall, its carpeting, flooring and curtains were supplied by Kean and Scott of Birmingham. Open from 9.30 a.m. to 4.30 p.m. Monday to Friday and from 9.30 a.m. to 12 noon on Saturdays, the office emphasised the major presence of the West Bromwich in Wales.[26]

Not all of the new branches were successful immediately, but there can be no doubt that the Dilkes policy of building the Society was an outstanding success. Those societies which failed to grow were taken over or were forced into mergers. The West Bromwich avoided this fate because of sound and perceptive management. By late 1978 it had sixty-seven branches. Their presence was most noticeable in West Bromwich itself, Birmingham, Warley, Dudley, mid and north Wales, and Shropshire – although there were also branches in Hampshire, Bedfordshire and elsewhere.[27] With assets of over £100 million, it ranked number twenty-five among building societies in the land. Larger than the Birmingham, Heart of England and Staffordshire Building Societies it was exceeded in the Midlands only by the Midshires, Coventry Economic and Derbyshire Building Societies. Though without the national presence or assets of societies such as the Abbey National and Provincial, the West Bromwich was in a secure and prosperous position.[28] Solid in its regional base, it was able to reject approaches to merge with both the Birmingham Midshires and the Woolwich.[29] Justifiably, Frank Dilkes was proud that the growth of the West Bromwich was unlike that of many other societies in that it occurred 'purely by our own efforts', without mergers or takeovers.[30]

Crucially, the West Bromwich did not forget its origins during this period of building the Society. Early in his presidency, Bernard Smith had proclaimed that 'we depend largely on the savings of the working classes'.[31] Intent upon staying true to its ideals, the West Bromwich collaborated with Birmingham Corporation on a major initiative aimed at making home ownership easier. According to Honorary Alderman Mrs. Freda Cocks, O.B.E., J.P.:

> When I was chairman of The Housing Committee of The Birmingham City Council in the 1960s & 1970s, we commenced selling council houses to those wishing to own homes. The West Bromwich Building Society were particularly helpful in supporting this initiative and if their archives have a reference to this I would be more than pleased to add a personal record of my thanks and congratulations . . .[32]

The bond between the West Bromwich and its traditional customers was made plain by Sue Barleet-Cross. She started work with the Society in 1976 as a cashier at the Great Barr branch and noticed that 'to many we were a working class "bank". Elderly customers used the Society to save for their funerals, others would just pop in for a chat and overall there was a close relationship with staff'.[33]

Nancy Oakley, was a cashier in the Lower Gornal branch, near Dudley, from its opening in 1977 until the branch closed in 1992.

She recalls how staff always went out of their way to make customers feel welcome.

'One customer always used to make us her last port of call because she knew she would come away with a smile on her face. We tried to make customers feel at home and if they wanted to stop and talk about anything we would always listen.'

Nancy remembers staff actually going into their own pockets to help customers out.

'I knew one customer was threatened with having her gas supply cut off. She had a cheque paid into her account waiting to clear but had no cash. She was recently widowed with young children, so I lent her the £40 she needed. As soon as her cheque cleared I was paid back.'

John Mees, then manager at the branch, also helped a loyal customer in a similar situation. John went to his own bank to withdraw £100 to lend to a customer, who on Christmas Eve desperately needed the money for the holiday period. When the branch reopened after the Christmas break the money was waiting for John in full.

The appreciation of customers was shown when Nancy was the victim of a robbery. Although she was not hurt, customers inundated her with cards and even some gifts after the raid.

As the branch network expanded so did the Society's technology although this was slow compared with the lightning speed of change in the 1990s. In the 1950s until the mid 1960s letters to savers and borrowers had to be addressed by hand until an automatic addressing machine was bought. To make interest calculations staff were helped by tables used as ready-reckoners, and later a handle-operated adding machine was allowed. With such important calculations staff were taught to be meticulous and talking about anything not work related in office time was forbidden.

Barrie Willetts joined the Society in 1969 as a forerunner of today's IT department and oversaw much of the change to a modern technology-driven organisation.

Until the late 1960s mechanical accounting machines were used for ledger cards and in 1968 the Society's first computer, an NCR visible records computer, was used for investment accounts. Ledger cards with four magnetic strips stored basic information such as the account number, balance and last transaction date.

All data was punched on to paper tape from receipt and withdrawal slips and the cards were then sorted and an account number list produced to store the cards in large fireproof cabinets.

Despite this technology it would still take more than one working day to record a day's transactions. In the early 1970s West Bromwich was again at the forefront of technology for building societies. With 17 other societies it used the Centre File Bureau System which stored data, transmitted via a telephone line, to a mainframe computer in London. Printouts of the data were delivered the next day.

Lauries Interest Tables.

215 Days   215

5%			4½%			4%			£	3½%			3%			2½%			¼%		
£	s	d	£	s	d	£	s	d		£	s	d	£	s	d	£	s	d	£	s	d
1	15	11¹	1	12	4	1	8	9	61	1	5	1³	1	1	6³	–	17	11²	–	1	9²
1	16	6¹	1	12	10¹	1	9	2²	62	1	5	6³	1	1	10³	–	18	3	–	1	10
1	17	1¹	1	13	4²	1	9	8¹	63	1	5	11²	1	2	3	–	18	6²	–	1	10¹
1	17	8²	1	13	11	1	10	2	64	1	6	4²	1	2	7²	–	18	10¹	–	1	10²
1	18	3¹	1	14	5¹	1	10	7²	65	1	6	9¹	1	2	11²	–	19	1²	–	1	11
1	18	10²	1	14	11³	1	11	1¹	66	1	7	2²	1	3	3³	–	19	5¹	–	1	11¹
1	19	5²	1	15	6	1	11	6³	67	1	7	7²	1	3	8	–	19	8³	–	1	11³
2	–	-³	1	16	-²	1	12	-²	68	1	8	-²	1	4	-¹	1	–	-¹	–	2	–
2	–	7³	1	16	6³	1	12	6	69	1	8	5¹	1	4	4²	1	–	3³	–	2	-¹
2	1	3	1	17	1¹	1	12	11³	70	1	8	10¹	1	4	9	1	–	7²	–	2	-³
2	1	9³	1	17	7²	1	13	5¹	71	1	9	3	1	5	1	1	–	10³	–	2	1
2	2	5	1	18	2	1	13	11	72	1	9	8¹	1	5	5¹	1	1	2²	–	2	1²
2	3	–	1	18	8²	1	14	4³	73	1	10	1¹	1	5	9²	1	1	6	–	2	1³
2	3	7	1	19	2³	1	14	10¹	74	1	10	6	1	6	1³	1	1	9²	–	2	2¹
2	4	2¹	1	19	9	1	15	4	75	1	10	11	1	6	6	1	2	1	–	2	2²
2	4	9	2	–	3¹	1	15	9²	76	1	11	3³	1	6	10	1	2	4²	–	2	2³
2	5	4¹	2	–	9³	1	16	3¹	77	1	11	9	1	7	2²	1	2	8	–	2	3¹
2	5	11¹	2	1	4	1	16	9	78	1	12	1³	1	7	6³	1	2	11²	–	2	3²
2	6	6²	2	1	10²	1	17	2³	79	1	12	6³	1	7	11	1	3	3¹	–	2	4
2	7	1²	2	2	4³	1	17	8¹	80	1	12	11³	1	8	3	1	3	6³	–	2	4¹
2	7	8³	2	2	11¹	1	18	2	81	1	13	4³	1	8	7²	1	3	10¹	–	2	4²
2	8	3²	2	3	5²	1	18	7³	82	1	13	9²	1	8	11³	1	4	1³	–	2	5
2	8	10³	2	4	–	1	19	1²	83	1	14	2³	1	9	4	1	4	5¹	–	2	5¹
2	9	5³	2	4	6¹	1	19	7	84	1	14	7²	1	9	8¹	1	4	8³	–	2	5³
2	10	-³	2	5	-²	2	–	-²	85	1	15	-²	1	10	-¹	1	5	-¹	–	2	6
2	10	8	2	5	7	2	–	6¹	86	1	15	5²	1	10	4²	1	5	4	–	2	6²
2	11	3	2	6	1¹	2	–	11³	87	1	15	10¹	1	10	9	1	5	7²	–	2	6³
2	11	10	2	6	7³	2	1	5²	88	1	16	3¹	1	11	1¹	1	5	11	–	2	7
2	12	5	2	7	2	2	1	11	89	1	16	8¹	1	11	5¹	1	6	2²	–	2	7²
2	13	-¹	2	7	8²	2	2	4³	90	1	17	1¹	1	11	9²	1	6	6	–	2	7³
2	13	7¹	2	8	3	2	2	10²	91	1	17	6¹	1	12	2	1	6	9²	–	2	8¹
2	14	2²	2	8	9¹	2	3	4¹	92	1	17	11¹	1	12	6¹	1	7	1¹	–	2	8²
2	14	9¹	2	9	3²	2	3	9³	93	1	18	4	1	12	10¹	1	7	4²	–	2	8³
2	15	4¹	2	9	9³	2	4	3¹	94	1	18	9	1	13	2²	1	7	8	–	2	9¹
2	15	11²	2	10	4¹	2	4	9	95	1	19	2	1	13	6³	1	7	11³	–	2	9²
2	16	6²	2	10	10²	2	5	2³	96	1	19	6³	1	13	11	1	8	3¹	–	2	10
2	17	1³	2	11	5	2	5	8²	97	1	19	11³	1	14	3¹	1	8	6³	–	2	10¹
2	17	8³	2	11	11¹	2	6	2	98	2	–	4³	1	14	7²	1	8	10¹	–	2	10²
2	18	3³	2	12	5³	2	6	7³	99	2	–	9³	1	14	11³	1	9	1³	–	2	11
2	18	10³	2	13	–	2	7	1²	100	2	1	2³	1	15	4	1	9	5¹	–	2	11¹
5	17	9²	5	6	-¹	4	14	3	200	4	2	5²	3	10	8¹	2	18	10³	–	5	10³
8	16	8³	7	19	-²	7	1	4¹	300	6	3	8²	5	6	-¹	4	8	4¹	–	8	10
11	15	7²	10	12	-²	9	8	5³	400	8	4	11	7	1	4¹	5	17	9³	–	11	9¹
14	14	6¹	13	5	-³	11	15	7¹	500	10	6	2	8	16	8²	7	7	3	–	14	8³
17	13	5	15	18	-³	14	2	8³	600	12	7	4²	10	12	-²	8	16	8²	–	17	8
20	12	3³	18	11	1	16	9	10	700	14	8	7²	12	7	4²	10	6	1³	1	–	7¹
23	11	3	21	4	1¹	18	16	11³	800	16	9	10¹	14	2	9	11	15	7²	1	3	6³
26	10	1³	23	17	1²	21	4	1¹	900	18	11	1	15	18	1	13	5	-³	1	6	6
29	9	-²	26	10	1²	23	11	2³	1000	20	12	3³	17	13	5	14	14	6¹	1	9	5²
58	18	1	53	–	3	47	2	5²	2000	41	4	7³	35	6	10	29	9	-²	2	18	10³
88	7	1²	79	10	4³	70	13	8¹	3000	61	16	11³	53	–	3	44	3	6³	4	8	4¹
117	16	2	106	–	6²	94	4	11	4000	82	9	3²	70	13	8¹	58	18	1	5	17	9³
147	5	2²	132	10	8¹	117	16	2	5000	103	1	7³	88	7	1²	73	12	7¹	7	7	3
176	14	3	159	–	9²	141	7	4²	6000	123	13	11²	106	–	4²	88	7	1²	8	16	8²
206	3	3¹	185	10	11¹	164	18	7²	7000	144	6	3¹	123	13	11²	103	1	7³	10	6	2
235	12	3³	212	1	1	188	9	10	8000	164	18	7²	141	7	4²	117	16	1³	11	15	7¹
265	1	4¹	238	11	2³	212	1	1	9000	185	10	11¹	159	–	9²	132	10	8	13	5	-³
294	10	5	265	1	4¹	235	12	3³	10000	206	3	3¹	176	14	3	147	5	2²	14	14	6¹
589	–	9³	530	2	8³	471	4	7³	20000	412	6	6³	353	8	5³	294	10	4³	29	9	-²

AUGUST 3rd.—150 Days to 31st of December.

30 May

A New Principal Office

In 1978 operations were moved from the Home of Thrift, which has since been used as a branch, to a 'new multi-million pound administration block' which was regarded as taking the Society 'into the year 2000 and beyond with confidence to face the future'. Expanding business had led to more staff and to cramped conditions in the old offices. This problem was compounded by various systems of working, which were 'not at all conducive to efficient administration'. With an annual growth rate of 22½%, the need for a move had been recognised by Frank Dilkes in the early 1970s, and at first it was planned to build on a back street site. However, it was soon realised that the amount of extra office space would not

The new Principal Office of West Bromwich Building Society,
on the corner of High Street and Dartmouth Street, 1978.

justify the proposed expenditure and fortunately a better position became available. Located on the corner of High Street and Dartmouth Street it was bought at a modest price because of the mid-1970s slump in land values. The builders, Bryant's, began work in July 1976 and work was finished in October 1978. The move to the new Principal Office was affectionately known as Operation Beaver and staff were given the opportunity to visit the building during construction to acquaint themselves with their new environment. Prior to the big move staff were also given a welcome pack of stationery which even included an ashtray.

The booklet 'An Introduction To 374 High Street', distributed to all staff showed that the Society was keen to show its new building off to staff and their families.

'It is intended that we should arrange as soon as we sensibly can Open Nights for Husbands, Wives and Parents, so that members of staff can proudly display all the facilities that are available.'

An aerial view of Principal Office.

Designed by the Hurley Robinson Partnership, this new Principal Office originally had five floors and part way through the construction it was agreed to insert an extra floor to accommodate future growth. The new offices had air conditioning, open-plan offices, a special computer area and a room in which the deeds to 'a staggering 150,000 homes can be stored'.[35] Costing £2.5 million to build and £150,000 a year to maintain, the expenditure was justified by Frank Dilkes. Deputy Chairman of the board as well as managing director, he believed that the offices would 'mean a better service and more efficiency', whilst they would also 'enable us to bring departments such as valuations, premises and branches under one roof for the first time, which will mean better communications'. There was even a special sound-proofed area 'so that the noisy job of producing computer punch cards can be carried out without affecting other staff'.[36]

As a modernistic structure the Principal Office did not have the classical dignity of the Home of Thrift, but it did provide employees with better facilities such as coffee areas, conference rooms, a canteen and a recreation area. The building was designed to cope with the Society's rapid expansion and shortly after its opening much of the new office space remained unused. The building's third floor was unoccupied for at least six years and Frank Dilkes obtained a rebate for the business rates the Society paid.

John Kent worked in both buildings. Today John is the holder of the John Scott Wright watch given by the former managing director and secretary to the Society for presentation to the longest serving male employee. John was presented with the gold Hunter watch on the death of the previous holder Wilf Horton. The watch had originally been presented to Mr. Scott Wright by the Society. John joined the West Bromwich in 1968 as a mortgage clerk, hoping that he would have more time with his family. Aged thirty-one, he had moved to this position from the Sunhouse factory in Walsall where he had been a toolmaker. John's new job entailed the processing of mortgage applications, the interviewing of applicants, 'status checking' – usually by way of an employer's reference – and calculating monthly repayments. Like most other societies, the West Bromwich would not consider an advance on a house which would be more than sixty years old at the end of the mortgage term. Thus, in 1968 if an applicant was seeking a twenty-five year mortgage then the property would have to have been built in 1933 or after. This policy was enforced until about 1970.

The interviewing of applicants normally took place on a Saturday morning at 321, High Street – The Home of Thrift. John recalls the building as 'a rather dark place, with corridors and closed offices'. It provided a stark contrast with the Principal Office.

About fifty people worked at the head office. It had quite a Victorian feel with dingy corridors and a very smoky atmosphere because in those days virtually everybody smoked at their desks. At break times we used to have mugs of coffee brought to us on a tray by the caretaker. People were very excited about the new building. It was very modern and contemporary and

John Kent, holder of the John Scott Wright watch.

was the most striking building in the area. Before we had been working in small offices at Victorian desks and suddenly we were in an open plan office in an ultra-modern building with each department on a separate floor. The new building had a staff restaurant and before we only had a kitchen – we thought it was fantastic.[37]

Chef Ivor Marsh with assistants Carolyne Satchwell and Janice Meadows in the kitchens of the new Principal Office of West Bromwich Building Society, 1979. (by permission of Birmingham Evening Mail)

Offices in the new Principal Office of West Bromwich Building Society.

Along with the Personnel Department the new restaurant was the responsibility of Dr. Neil Whyte. Formerly a physicist, in 1979 he wrote an essay on how good food helps people to work better. It won him a £100 prize in a competition.[38] The same year he saved the Society over £2,000 by deciding to send its 170,000 statements through a bulk mail firm in Bradford, using the Post Office's rebate mail scheme.[39] But like all employees of the West Bromwich, Dr. Whyte had to be conversant and skilled in the main aspects of the Society's activities. In 1978 he was awarded three major prizes in the professional examinations set by The Chartered Building Societies Institute: for best student; for best student in English Land Law; and for best student in Housing & Planning. Michael Price, secretary of the West Bromwich, was also successful and gained the prize for the best student in building society management.[40] Professional awards were actively encouraged by Frank Dilkes, a man who was a longstanding director and Chairman of Fanhams Hall Companies – the Institute's national training centre.

Notable for its manufactured polished granite and gold solar glass, the new Principal Office was made more distinctive by a large mural in the reception hall. It was crafted by William Burgess, a former art teacher. Like those murals he had done for branches in St. Ives, Oswestry, Porthmadog and elsewhere, the

The superb mural depicting scenes from the history of West Bromwich and situated in the reception areas of the Society's new Principal Office, November 1978.

inspiration came from local history and stories. Using clay from Stoke-on-Trent, he etched his illustrations in relief, then baked them, glazed them and re-baked them 'to bring out the sparkling colours'. All this was done painstakingly in a kiln in the back garden of his Sedgley home. Consisting of six terracotta panels superimposed on flooring stone, the final mural represents the industry, commerce and history of West Bromwich.

At the top left is the Town Hall and an early Corporation bus standing in front of a modern motorway. The top right shows the gasometers of Swan Village, with which Reuben Farley was so associated. Centre right focuses on Hamstead Colliery with its winding gear, and a Great Western locomotive to indicate the significance of the Black Country to railway carriage construction. Lower right is dominated by the Oak House, again recalling Reuben Farley's contribution to the civic pride of West Bromwich and also harking back to the Turtons who once lived there and John Wesley who once preached there. Suitably placed in front is Farley's Clock Tower and the West Bromwich town crest. This represents the iron and brass industries and has the motto 'Labor Omnia Vincit' – 'Effort Overcomes All'.

On the bottom right the Dartmouth Square Clock is placed amongst a scene representing Salter's contribution to heavy industrial and personal weighing machines. The importance of the waterways is asserted on the bottom left by the cast iron Galton Bridge over the Birmingham Canal and a narrow boat. Named 'Broom' it signifies the wild broom which flowered on West Bromwich heath and from which the word Bromwich is derived. The mural is a wonderful work and a fitting tribute to the men and women who 'collared hard' to make West Bromwich the town of a hundred trades and who saved with their own building society. Finally the relevance of West Bromwich Albion to the history of the town and to football internationally is made plain by a footballer with the F.A. Cup, and marking the long connections between the club and the Society.

Chapter 5:

Independent and Strong, 1979-89

The West Bromwich continued to show spectacular results. In 1978 it increased its assets to £216 million, up by 19% on those of the year before. This gain was outstripped by only two other societies. The market leader remained the Halifax with huge assets of £7 billion, but within the Midlands only the Derbyshire was bigger than the West Bromwich – and that was by only a small margin.[1] These results were achieved despite the severe downturns in the economy which had bedevilled the 1970s. These had led to exceptionally high interest rates of 11% and had often caused drastic falls in the number of mortgage applications.[2]

For all these problems, there had been a persistent increase in the national percentage of owner-occupied houses. This stood at 46.6% in 1965, and following a golden age of the movement in the 1960s and 1970s the proportion had increased substantially to 54.6% by 1979.

It was unrealistic to expect this comfortable trading background to continue. Building societies basically provided services for savings and mortgages. With such a limited range of products they were vulnerable to potential competitors. This threat became a reality following the victory of the Conservative Party at the General Election of 1979. Led by Margaret Thatcher, an avowed free marketeer, the new government vigorously espoused policies aimed at deregulation and *laissez-faire*. Most pertinently, the banking system was opened up by legislation, 'in itself coinciding with a change of philosophy on the part of the banks which led them to enter the mortgage market. Shaken by new competition, building societies were further taken aback by the wish of the government to use National Savings to fund its borrowing requirements'.[3]

This led to the end of the cartel that building societies had previously enjoyed. Paradoxically these developments arose at the same time as the Conservatives were introducing laws which aimed to raise further the proportion of owner occupiers and reduce the number of council house tenants. This objective was to be attained in two ways: through the virtual ending of municipal house building and through the encouragement of tenants to buy the properties they rented via the 'Right to Buy' provisions in the Housing Act of 1980.

The early years of that decade were marked by continuing economic problems. In particular, borrowing was hindered badly by massive job losses and by a minimum lending rate which dropped too slowly from the abnormally high level of 16%. Still, the Conservative Party's determination to push forward with root and branch changes in government and society was reinforced by its victory in

A 1980s society gift voucher.

A gift to build on

WEST BROMWICH
BUILDING SOCIETY

The Society's new corporate image introduced in 1982. Pictured is the Walsall branch.

the General Election of 1984. Two years later another Building Societies Act was passed. This gave such bodies wider powers in the field of housing and allowed them to offer personal banking facilities, life assurance, pensions and estate agency services to their customers. With the Financial Services Act of the same year, the new legislation enabled building societies to become more effective in countering the intense competition they had faced from banks. They did this by pushing forward a strong image and introducing innovative products, especially in the field of mortgages.

In 1983 Bernard Smith retired as chairman of the West Bromwich. Then ninety-one years old, he intended to carry on as a director and in his work with solicitors William Bache and Sons.[4] He was succeeded by Frank Dilkes, who had recently retired as managing director. By this date the Society had introduced a new corporate image and West Bromwich boasted ninety branches and assets of £338 million. Importantly, it also had 250,000 investors, approximately 27,000 borrowing members, and it ranked twenty-fourth in size out of 218 building societies nationally.[5]

Under the chairmanship of Frank Dilkes, the West Bromwich forged ahead into new fields of business, a development that had been heralded even before

Coronation Street star Thelma Barlow, who played Mavis Riley, opens the Society's 87th branch in Caldmore Road, Walsall.

Bernard Smith's retirement plaque, 1983. (courtesy of Hilton Studios, Staffordshire)

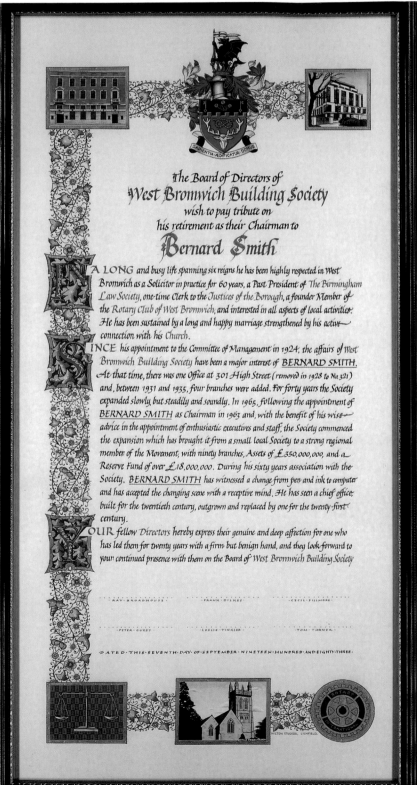

the 1986 Building Societies Act. Indeed, as early as 1978, Frank Dilkes had confirmed that in exceptional circumstances the West Bromwich was willing to lend money to existing borrowers for the purchase of cars and shares.[6] In the ensuing decade such loans were made more frequently, whilst a foreign currency service was introduced. These moves were just two of a number of initiatives which were taken by the 'cautiously modern and forward looking' Society as it strove to maintain and improve its position. In particular, in 1982, the West Bromwich led the way 'into a new field for building societies' by joining with the National Mutual Life Assurance Society to offer a pension scheme. This was 'tailored to the needs of the self-employed and to the many workers in small Black Country firms which do not have their own pension funds'. Under the scheme a minimum lump sum of £2,000 was paid for a pension bond which was invested in the West Bromwich. The interest which accrued was utilised to fund the premiums on a National Mutual pension policy.[7]

The West Bromwich forged another important link in 1986 when it entered into an agreement with the Britannic Assurance Company. In the following year

Frank Dilkes (right), Chairman of West Bromwich Building Society, and Michael Willett, Chairman of Britannic Assurance, celebrating the link up between the two institutions in 1986.

the Society would provide £25 million, a fifth of its current lending, to be offered 'on the doorstep' via the insurance field staff who worked from the Britannic's sixty district offices in the West Midlands and Wales. In return, the West Bromwich would use its branches in the same regions to sell Britannic endowment schemes and other policies alongside those of three other leading companies. According to Frank Dilkes, the tie-up was 'the most cost-effective way of retaining a competitive edge', enabling each company to concentrate on its individual area of expertise and avoid the duplication of activities. The West Bromwich could only enter into such an agreement because of recent legislation which also enabled it to go into house contents insurance in 1988 with the launch of Coversure,[8] a competitive home and contents insurance package, which offered various levels of cover.

Regional offices of Britannic were used as collecting agents for the Society to help attract new investment accounts. Within the next two years, the relationship with the Britannic was ended amicably; an insurance consultancy team was formed to develop custom in life assurance, pensions, investment bonds, unit trusts and medical insurance services; 16 district managers were appointed to improve business in the eighty-one branches.[9]

The new West Bromwich Building Society Insurance Consultancy team. From the left: John Clarke, Gill Lavill, Andy Heseltine and Leigh Gardner, 1989.

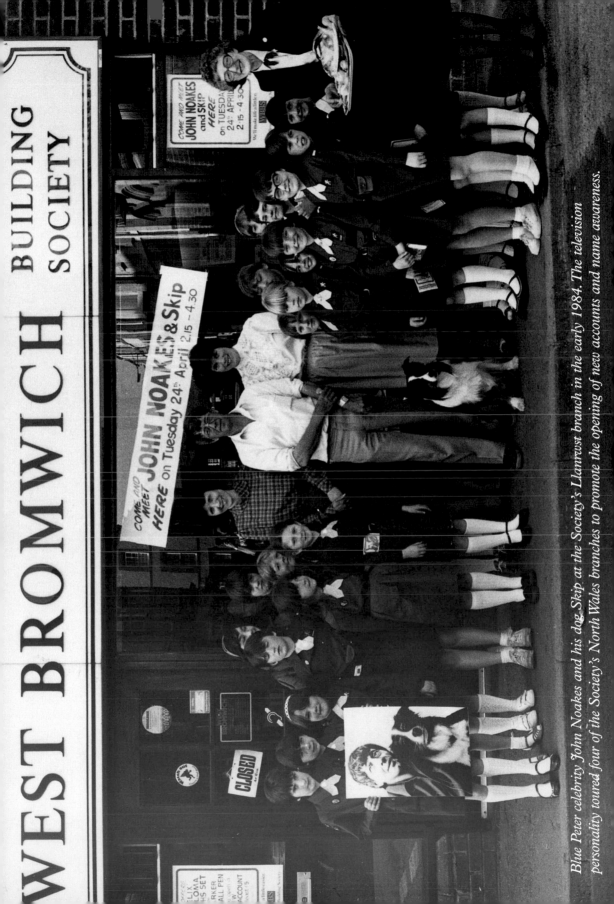

Blue Peter celebrity John Noakes and his dog Skip at the Society's Llanrwst branch in the early 1984. The television personality toured four of the Society's North Wales branches to promote the opening of new accounts and name awareness.

As in the past, new moves by the West Bromwich did not mean that the Society ignored its traditional responsibilities. In 1980 it responded positively to an appeal made by striking Black Country steel workers that their mortgage payments be suspended, leaving them to pay the interest only during the dispute. As Leslie Tinkler emphasised, 'in such cases where men find they are suddenly without an income we always try to be as sympathetic as we can'.[10] Two years later the Society successfully built on the connection which it had established with Councillor Freda Cocks and Birmingham City Council in the 1970s. The Society offered 100% mortgages to those of the corporation's tenants who wished to buy their homes – with the bonus that valuation and solicitor's fees would be added to the sum advanced. As a result some rent-payers were able to make a purchase without putting down a deposit, subject to having an income sufficient to meet repayments. Applicants were able to borrow up to three times the amount of their income; whilst in cases where both husband and wife were working, the whole of the lower income could be considered. The West Bromwich helped up to 200 tenants to buy their houses in Birmingham with advances of £2 million. Similar funds were allotted the next year, when the Society made it plain that it had 'money available to help other applicants wanting to buy a home of their own'.[11]

The innovative approach of the Society to its products was matched by exciting developments in its day-to-day operations. In 1982 the West Bromwich embarked on a programme of installing terminals in branches so that they might be connected with the ICL mainframe computer at Head Office. Nixdorf Computer Limited was chosen to supply the equipment. The company used COBOL as its language, the same as that already adopted by the West Bromwich. Consequently, the Society was able to design and programme the system according to its own requirements. The first terminals were rolled out in the branches in Dartmouth Square and 321 High Street in West Bromwich and Great Bridge and Handsworth and by the end of the 1980s this 'counter top technology network' was in all eighty-one branches. It could transmit all transactions at the end of the day and process them overnight. Staff were trained in using the new equipment. The effect was impressive. Staff could swiftly and efficiently make enquiries about balances and account details at branches rather than having to telephone the computer room at Principal Office.[12] The advantages were highlighted by Malcolm Smith, a member of the steering committee for the implementation of the programme:

> The major factor is, I suggest, service to customers. All other benefits contribute towards this main aim . . . The whole point of having a computer is that you have a sophisticated tool to help with a large number of problems. Very similar to a farmer using a combine harvester. Computer equipment will give Branch Staff more time to talk to customers by reducing paperwork to a minimum. This is how it should be. The principal function of a Branch ought to be as the workforce of a marketing operation and not as administrators. There will, of course, always be administrative matters to deal with but Branch work will become far more satisfying for Staff if routine tasks are kept to a minimum.[13]

The renovated offices of the former headquarters of the West Bromwich Building Society, 1981. In the background is the Society's first ever in-branch computer, an ICL, which could handle simple customer enquiries. The information could be seen only on-screen and no printouts were available.

Frank Dilkes (left, Chairman of West Bromwich Building Society, and Richard Lawson, Chairman of Smith Keen Cutler Limited and former Deputy Chairman of the Stock Exchange, celebrating the opening of the Wolverhampton Share Shop in the Victoria branch of the Society, 15 October 1987.

The Society's Merry Hill branch showing the logo introduced in 1982.

This installation of computers was accompanied by the ongoing improvement of all premises used by the West Bromwich. In 1981 the former headquarters at 321 High Street were completely renovated and refurbished. The work was undertaken to make the building, now the Society's senior branch office, brighter and more modern, to improve efficiency and to bring a better service to investors and borrowers.[14] Two years later, the West Bromwich unveiled 'a "breakthrough" in the design of the interior of building society branches'. After a successful pilot at its premises in Manchester, 'a revolutionary new open plan' was adopted for the West Bromwich branch at 166A Alcester Road, Moseley. This did away with 'the austere security arrangements which have traditionally forced a barrier between a society and its members'. Wall-to-wall counters and high security screens disappeared and were replaced by 'a much more informal layout'. According to Leslie Tinkler, then managing director of the West Bromwich, this meant that 'people can walk in, sit down, and discuss money matters in a relaxed and comfortable atmosphere'. Security matters were not ignored in this pioneering open plan. Through the careful positioning of the cashiers and other staff, the Society was confident that safety had actually been improved.[15]

Security had become an important consideration. Once unheard of, robberies of building society branches were now one of the negative aspects of the social changes wrought since the early 1960s. The West Bromwich was not exempt from this unfortunate trend and in September 1975, Dennis Troth, manager of the Erdington branch, showed 'great courage' in chasing off a raider who had

New look branches – Denton branch.

demanded cash.[16] His example was followed by many of the Society's staff. In August 1985, Sandra Needham stayed calm when three men threatened her with 'a realistic imitation pistol'. A cashier, Sandra told the thieves that there was no money in her Sedgley branch. At the subsequent trial of the three offenders, the judge praised her 'remarkable loyalty to her firm'.[17] Within two months similar bravery was shown by Tony Dubberley, then manager of the High Street, Smethwick branch, when he 'pounced on a raider and wrestled the gun from his hand'. In spite of the kicks, punches and bites of the robber, the manager succeeded in detaining his assailant. He was helped by his assistant and a male customer.[18]

Such crimes induced Wolverhampton Borough Council in 1982 to serve an enforcement order on the West Bromwich to put up 'bandit-proof' screens in its branch at Lichfield Street in the town. The Society contested the enforcement, asserting that it would mean spending £500,000 on installing the screens in all its branches. Moreover, it was argued that the screens offered no deterrent to robbers whilst they would end the 'friendly and relaxed atmosphere' in branches.

Staff at the West Smethwick branch just after its refurbishment in 1984.
Left to Right: Janet Gobele, John Davies, Tony Dubberley and Irene Whitehead.

*The revolutionary open-plan of the Moseley branch (Birmingham)
of West Bromwich Building Society.*

In 1982 an industrial tribunal ruled in favour of the council, although its findings were reversed in the High Court.[19] This last decision was welcomed not only by the West Bromwich but also by The Building Societies Association.[20]

In keeping with the aims and principles of its founders, throughout this period of rapid change and growth the West Bromwich adhered to a belief that it owed a duty to its members and the communities from which it had grown. This commitment was reflected in a variety of ways. In 1980 the window of the High Street, Harborne branch was given over to pupils from Bartley Green School for them to dress it with arts and crafts; the next year the High Street, Erdington branch presented a giant Christmas cake to the disabled children of the Bridge School.[21] Then at the flagship 321 High Street branch in West Bromwich, David ran in the Sandwell Pancake Day Race. Organised by radio station BRMB and the Birmingham Evening Mail local traders and business people would race down West Bromwich High Street, tossing pancakes as they ran.

David and fellow 321 member Bob Hardie took part and the Society won the coveted prize – a copper-bottomed frying pan that was proudly displayed in the branch.

Another of his ideas was to transform part of the foyer area of 321 with an oche and dartboard as David completed a one man darts marathon for local charity the Chest Care Association in March 1985.

For seven hours and twenty minutes David threw darts non-stop, making more than 4,500 throws and scoring more than 66,000 points. The one time pub league darts player recorded one 180, twenty bullseyes and fifty-nine scores of more than 100.

During the 1980s David Hill was one of the Society's managers who was actively promoting the West Bromwich name through community activities. Above with Leslie Tinkler and a representative of the Chest Care Association after his darts marathon, and below warming up with Bob Hardie, his assistant, for the Sandwell Evening Mail Pancake Day race. (below: with permission of Birmingham Evening Mail)

But perhaps the most important statistic was the £600 he raised for the Chest Care Association with customers' help.

A year later the staff at the Stratford Road, Hall Green branch arranged for Father Christmas to pop into their office to meet local youngsters; whilst the employees at the Villa Road, Lozells branch staged an exhibition of the work of the Afro-Caribbean artist, Pogus Caesar.[22]

The Society itself organised a number of major fund-raising ventures for charity, such as the Piles of Pennies Competition. Initiated in 1980, within three years it involved 160 Black Country pubs. In each of them the regulars built money mountains in the hope of raising £10,000 for local blind people. The top dozen pubs were visited by celebrities including Coronation Street's Eddie Yates, actor Geoff Hughes, and Mavis Riley, actress Thelma Barlow, who knocked over the huge piles of pennies. In 1982 the competition was won by the

Coronation Street's jovial dustman Eddie Yates (actor Geoff Hughes) with the promotions team, at the opening of the Society's High Street, Tipton branch, 1982. More than 200 people turned out to greet him in November 1982.

'King's Arms' in Tipton. The next year the West Bromwich Building Society Cup was awarded to the 'White Horse', Wednesbury whose customers raised £660 through raffles, barbecues, a Halloween fancy dress and a streak by a mystery masked bachelor.[23] Involvement has also been noticeable in causes targeted at children and young people. In 1984 and in co-operation with the then West Midlands County Council, the West Bromwich designed 'The Language of the Road' campaign. This aimed to help children understand the different road signs and symbols. Leaflets were handed out, teaching aids were provided and road safety projects were set up.[24]

Ron Sergeant, Promotions Manager, spreads the word at a show in Stourbridge 1982.

Ron Sergeant and Angela Paskin on a Christmas branch promotion 1983.
The team visited eighteen branches in the eleven days before Christmas.

As a mutual society founded by its members for its members, the West Bromwich is readier than many organisations to be regularly involved in good causes. Yet though it does not make a profit as such, it is imperative for its present and future well-being that the Society ensures that income exceeds expenditure. This can be achieved only if sufficient customers are attracted. Accordingly, in a fiercely competitive market the West Bromwich has to keep its name in the public eye. A promotions manager, Ron Sergeant, was appointed and a marketing strategy developed which centred on promotional activities in branches and the communities served by the Society. A promotions vehicle was bought and taken to county shows such as the Three Counties and the Royal Show as well as the Sandwell Show and other community events involving, for example, scout groups and the Road Safety Authority. Marketing initiatives were also launched at branches, like the 'Name the Place' competition of 1982. First prize was a weekend for two in Paris. As explained by Angela Paskin, now branch

The folk of the 'White Horse', Wednesbury receiving the West Bromwich Building Society Cup for raising the most money in the Pile of Pennies competition raising money for charity. Leslie Tinkler, Managing Director of the Society is holding the cup, 1983. (by permission of Birmingham Evening Mail)

manager at Wednesbury, the aim of the competition was that members of the public and the Society should guess the location of photographs placed in branch windows:

> To create a visual interest, the Promotions Manager, Ron Sergeant and myself dressed up as a French couple, complete with old bicycle, onions and French bread. We even had French music playing underneath the onions and French sticks in the bicycle's basket. Ron rode this dangerous contraption 100 yards towards the Branch with me sitting in the basket, holding on for dear life! Dave Mackay who was the Society's Sales Manager at the time was our chauffeur and drove us and the bicycle around in a transit van, to all our destinations. My reputation has never been the same since those black fishnet stockings and Ron's moustache kept falling off when he tried his French accent, 'Ollo, ollo 'ere is a competition form – you feel it in and I weel give you a French kees.' On the Branch's busiest days, Friday, Saturday and Monday, the rest of the promotions team would join us to promote the competition. Many new accounts were opened for all the branches involved.[25]

Ron Sergeant and Angela Paskin with Warwick branch manager Peter Rule in 1982's Name the Place promotion.

Despite stiff competition from banks, the West Bromwich grew strongly in the early and mid-1980s. It was not alone. Many building societies benefited from the seemingly unstoppable surge in home ownership. Although over three million people were out of work for much of this period, many of those with jobs were enjoying unprecedented prosperity. By July 1986, inflation had dropped to a low of 2½% and real wages were rising. These circumstances made home ownership increasingly attractive – and house prices were rising at the unparalleled rate of 30% a year. Typically a three-bedroom semi detached house in the West Midlands increased in value from £25,000 in the late 1970s to £50,000 when the property

Jean George manager of the Walsall branch is presented with her Certificate in Building Societies Practice from Mark Boléat, Deputy Director-General of the Building Societies Association in 1985.

market peaked in the late 1980s. Acknowledging the boom in property values, most building societies were happy to meet the huge demand for mortgages. The West Bromwich was no exception.

In recognition of the progress made by the Society during this period and for his service to the Building Society movement as a whole, Chairman Frank Dilkes was made an OBE in the 1989 New Year's Honours List. His award was to prove a high point for the Society.

Frank Dilkes at Buckingham Palace to receive his OBE in 1989, accompanied by his wife Audrey, son Paul and daughter Teresa.

Chapter 6:

Mutuality Abounds – 1990-96

Worst Recession in Living Memory

In the favourable market conditions of the 1980s under the then Chief Executive Jeffrey Allard, who had joined from the Portsmouth Building Society in 1988, the West Bromwich embarked on a further period of expansion. In common with many societies at that time, it did so by relaxing its lending criteria and introducing new, untried, niche products including equity release mortgages. But this decision could not have been worse timed.

The economic situation deteriorated drastically from 1989 onwards, leading to the worst recession in living memory. Boom turned to bust in the property market, interest rates rose to more than 15%, with the Society's own mortgage rate peaking at 15.4%; unemployment rose rapidly as the economic downturn caused companies to reduce staff or simply to go out of business; and demand for owner-occupier housing plummeted. As a consequence property prices fell by as much as 40% and some borrowers were caught in a trap – unable to service the interest payments on their mortgage and unable, too, to sell their homes to clear the mortgage. A new phenomenon of 'negative equity', where the property was worth less than the borrower's mortgage, became a sadly common reality for many.

Building societies were compelled to come to terms with the rising numbers of borrowers who could not meet their mortgage repayments. Coupled with the ill-timed relaxation of lending criteria, the Society was hit harder than most and was set to face its sternest task yet - survival. Many building societies did not survive – in just five years, the number of societies fell from 126 to 96. Possessions of mortgaged properties rose to unprecedented levels throughout the industry. In 1989 figures from the Council of Mortgage lenders showed more than 80,000 mortgage accounts in arrears and 15,000 borrowers who had lost possession of their homes. Two years later, the number in arrears had swollen to 275,000 and possessions had escalated to 75,540.

Societies were forced to widen margins – the gap between the interest paid to savers and the interest charged to borrowers – and many, including the West Bromwich, had to streamline operations and cut costs. For the first time in its history the Society was forced to shed staff and rationalise the way it did business. Part of this painful but very necessary process was the closure of branches, shrinking the network mainly back to its Black Country heartland though it

Glenn Elliot, Chief Executive 1991-1996.

retained a significant presence in the West Midlands. The recession was to cause the most difficult trading conditions in the Society's long history. Its aftermath would be felt for many years to come.

The Road to Recovery

The West Bromwich recovery story began with the appointment of Glenn Elliot, a chartered accountant, as chief executive in 1991. An affable character with a natural ability to motivate people, he realised a long battle lay ahead and that additional expertise and skills would be required at senior management level to ensure survival. The Society had to focus on restoring prudent lending, reducing arrears, and returning to the principles of sound management, which had underpinned its success in the past. A number of executives and senior managers were recruited at this crucial time, notably Gary Cowdrill (Finance and Accounting), Philip Dearing (Sales), David Johnston (Marketing) and Richard Early (Commercial Lending). Combining with the existing management skills of David Mackay (Arrears), Paul Turner (Customer Services) and Tony Dubberley (Branch Operations) they set about tackling these critical tasks.

A major influence, too, was Andrew Messenger, who was appointed in 1991 as Deputy General Manager Lending with the vital responsibilities of restoring mortgage quality and tackling arrears. Rising later to become Chief Executive, he recalled those difficult days:

> 'We were in a recession with the worst arrears of any building society. It's no exaggeration to say we were on our knees. The fact that we weren't forced out of business or swallowed up is a success story in itself.'

In an interview with the *Express and Star* Andrew brought to mind how the staff joined him and others in management to tackle the staggering depth of debt, which totalled £70 million. Residual mortgage debts were so huge because of the recession, and with interest rates being so high people couldn't cope.'

Things were so bad that, according to Andrew, 'we would find house keys pushed through our letter box – often with no tag to say what house they belonged to. People just packed up and went and left the house because they simply couldn't afford to stay.'[1]

An experienced lender, who had held senior positions with a number of major banks and building societies, Andrew immediately harnessed the skills and efforts of those around him, introduced a new and comprehensive lending policy and brought in initiatives to help borrowers who had arrears problems, ensuring such people had access to prompt and sympathetic counselling. Often this was given outside normal working hours for the convenience of customers. The new approach brought immediate results, especially in arrears improvement, and was encapsulated by the heading printed on the new lending policy document. It read 'Quality will not be sacrificed for Quantity'. Andrew's success in the area of lending was accompanied by progress on other fronts under Glenn Elliot's leadership, such as the provision of crucial management information and the development of computer systems to remove the excessive burden of administration.

In 1991 the Society had passed the £1 billion asset milestone. However, the low point of the Society came the next year. Its insurers refused to pay out the Society's bad debt claims; there was a court case looming that would eventually

A competition to celebrate the Society reaching £1 billion assets in 1991. The first prize was £2,500.

cost many millions of pounds. Observers gave the Society six months to survive. It did more than that. It thrived, thanks to focused and experienced leadership, a clear and practical plan to move forward and an enormous amount of effort by everyone at the Society.

To publicise its sense of belief and purpose, in 1993 the West Bromwich brought out a distinctive oak tree symbol as its new corporate identity. This was introduced to improve the Society's profile by conveying its traditional values, strength and the safety it represented for investors. The logo was also used to give a more modern look to its branches - all of which were included in a pro-

The logo and fascia of the Leicester Mortgage Bureau.

gramme of refurbishment. The same year the first of the Society's Mortgage
Bureaux was opened in Manchester and, following its success, further Bureaux
were launched in Chester, Leicester, Cardiff, Coventry and Swindon. It was the
aim of the Bureaux to extend the Society's mortgage operation to strategic city
locations across the United Kingdom. In addition, the Society re-entered the
commercial loans market with the recruitment of a small team of specialist
commercial lenders to provide long-term finance to established businesses and
housing associations.

The pace of recovery and development continued in 1994 when the West
Bromwich won *What Mortgage* magazine's award as the best regional lender for
the best value mortgages. The progress made by the Society was clear and
prospects were much brighter, especially now that unemployment, interest rates
and inflation were falling.

*Cardiff Mortgage Bureau manager Maria Saunders makes a £500 donation to
Jeremy Beadle, President of the Children with Leukemia charity, with help from
Alan Darlow of Darlow's Estate Agency. The money was raised through the
Society's Community Counts Programme.*

Improving Efficiency and Controlling Costs

But the extra activity, people and effort, occasioned by the investment in new and necessary systems, saw costs rise dramatically. In 1992 John Baker, a director since 1984, was appointed Chairman, succeeding Thomas Turner. A chartered accountant, magistrate and former chairman of the Walsall Chamber of Commerce, John Baker was a strong-willed individual, who recognised the progress being made while also seeing the need for productivity enhancements and cost reduction. This was to result in branch closures, redundancies and rationalisation of the business.

Thomas Turner, seated, the Chairman of West Bromwich Building Society with his Deputy Chairman, John Baker, in 1990. Mr. Turner was described by Chief Executive of the Society Glenn Elliot as a 'giant of a man'.

John Baker recalled: 'The Building Society Act of 1986 not only strengthened the regulations by which building societies were bound but it also triggered the start of intense competition, exposing the need for them to become more efficient. When I became Chairman in 1992 the Society was an active and progressive organisation but it needed to invest in new technology, close unprofitable branches, streamline its administration and introduce new sources of income. It was a tough time for the staff and also for the directors, who knew such changes were vital if the Society was to remain independent and competitive in the 21st century.'

From 1992 to his retirement in 1998, the Society made very significant progress on a number of fronts. The management expense ratio fell by 35% from 1.93% to 1.26%, underlying pre-tax profits rose from £11.7 million to £20 million, and capital reserves increased from £89 million to £136 million.

Mayor of Sandwell John Sullivan, HRH Prince Edward and Chairman John Baker on the Prince's visit to Principal Office in 1993. He was presented with a £5,000 donation to launch the Duke of Edinburgh award scheme at West Bromwich Albion, supported by the Society.

Part of the Society's strong growth was achieved through the acquisition of mortgage portfolios. The Society had set up West Bromwich Mortgage Company Limited in 1995 to oversee this and by March 1998, the Company's assets exceeded £230 million - equivalent in size to the 37th largest building society in its own right. The Society's recovery and obvious progress attracted extensive support from the City. Evidence of this came in 1994 when the Society secured a £100 million syndicated loan to help fund West Bromwich Mortgage Company's first portfolio acquisition. Twenty major world banks funded the loan, emphasising their confidence in the Society.

Mutuality

Abbey National abandoned its mutual status in July 1989, ceasing to be a building society, citing the prescriptive regime of the 1986 Building Societies Act and the need to have access to capital as the key reasons. Many societies were expected to follow and though this took until 1995 to gather pace, the building society movement as a whole was badly harmed by further defections. In 1995, the Cheltenham and Gloucester Building Society became part of Lloyds Bank, whilst the Halifax and Leeds Permanent Building Societies merged and announced the intention to become a plc.

Around this time a new phenomenon arose - carpet bagging. Speculators rushed to open accounts with any building society in the hope that it would convert to a bank or be taken over. They could then claim 'free windfall' shares in the newly-converted organisation. As Andrew Messenger stressed 'these moves were unwelcome, irrational, impractical and extremely costly diversions' and he urged all members 'to repel the greed of these carpetbaggers, whose motives seek to deprive future generations of their mutual inheritance'. Unhappily the activity of the carpetbaggers was fuelled further in 1997 when, as expected, the Halifax shed its mutual status but also the Woolwich, Alliance & Leicester and the Northern Rock became banks. Similarly the Bristol & West Building Society joined the rush by agreeing to a takeover by Bank of Ireland.

Reacting to the individualistic self-centred attitudes of the carpetbaggers John Baker issued a powerful message about the future of the West Bromwich:

'Never have building societies experienced such disruption from rumour, speculation, and an uncharacteristic stampede by some to surrender the basic principles on which they were formed; the principles which enabled them to serve their members successfully for generations. As a Society, we are bound to act in the long term interests of all our members and not take a short term view which may seem attractive at a particular time. The dual combination of mutuality and independence enables us to provide optimum security for all our members and to make a growing contribution to the broader aspects of life in the community we serve.'[2]

Like the West Bromwich, many societies readily recognised that their members' best interests were served by remaining mutual and fought back strongly. Measures were put in place to protect businesses from carpetbaggers. The West Bromwich and others introduced higher minimum investment levels for new investors and placed restrictions on investments for those who lived outside the Society's heartland.

Steps to defend mutuality were matched by strong business performances by building societies so that, by 1996, they were taking more than their expected market share in both savings and mortgages. This trend was stressed in the Building Societies Commission Annual Review in 1997-98. It highlighted the fact that 'building societies were increasingly able to demonstrate to their members the tangible benefits of mutual status by way of more attractive interest rates to borrowers and savers, and loyalty bonuses. Importantly, building societies were quick to show that they did not have a service shareholder capital as did a plc and were thus empowered to narrow their net interest margins.'

As for the West Bromwich its illustrious history was built around mutuality – helping members, staff and the community to better themselves and it was determined to deliver this ideal. The Society was now well on the road to recovery and, as the Millennium approached, it was poised to leap forward in a stunning fashion.

Chapter 7:

Mutuality, the Millennium and Beyond

Sharing Success

The principle of mutuality has been the foundation stone of the West Bromwich since its beginnings and that principle was passionately defended and strengthened by Andrew Messenger, a man whose verve, vision, and campaigning led the West Bromwich to unparalleled achievements as the Society entered the new millennium. Appointed to the Board in 1995, just four years after he had joined the Society, he followed Glenn Elliott as Chief Executive in 1996. Crucially, Andrew was as much committed to improving the lives and enhancing the opportunities of ordinary citizens as had been the founders of the Society. His outstanding success lay in his ability to discern and react positively to changing circumstances, coupled with an unswerving determination to make the Society a proactive body that strove tirelessly for the well being of its members, staff and of the wider community as a whole.

Chief Executive, Andrew Messenger, makes a special presentation to local MP Betty Boothroyd to commemorate her retirement as Speaker of the House of Commons.

Proud of his working-class background and the youngest of four children, Andrew Messenger was raised in a council house in Sandbach, Cheshire. Not wanting to be a financial burden on his parents, he did not pursue a university education, despite gaining three top grades at 'A' level, but instead found work in a bank.

As his career in finance developed he constantly bore in mind the day-to-day worries of working families and the importance of saving – concerns that drew on his own experiences as a youngster, as he reveals in this episode:

'The man from the Pru (Prudential Insurance) called every Friday night. He always came after my dad had eaten his meal and had handed his wage packet - unopened - to my mother. I remember her upset because a rug she had saved up to buy was burnt after a piece of coal fell out of the fire. Then came this magic moment - that's how I saw it - when the insurance man said she could have another one. That was why she had been paying him every week.'

It was not an easy road to the top. Like many blessed with a regional accent, Andrew faced prejudice and ignorance. On one occasion, he was told by a Natwest bank executive that he would 'never get anywhere with that accent.' If anything, this made Andrew adhere proudly to his northern accent. Spurred on by a desire to succeed and to help others similarly achieve their aspirations, Andrew's career saw him amass 27 years experience with major banks and building societies, culminating in his appointment as Chief Executive of the West Bromwich in 1996.

Statement of Intent

Despite the genuine progress made in the previous five years there was still a daunting job ahead, as Andrew emphasised: 'I told everybody we had to cut arrears to a third, costs down a third, quadruple sales, double in size and triple profits and lending. Looking back, I set some over-ambitious goals. I was to learn that a motivated team was all powerful and could achieve almost anything.'[1]

Recognising that mutuality had been integral to the Society throughout its history and had, indeed, enabled the West Bromwich to provide better mortgage and investment rates than its banking competitors, the Society re-affirmed its allegiance to the principles and practice of mutuality in 1997. This consisted of a renewed statement of the Society's vision, which encapsulated its very purpose: Growing – Thriving – Sharing with members, staff and community.

In a six-point commitment constructed around the Society's core values, Andrew Messenger pledged that the West Bromwich would provide:

- Value-for-money products and services
- Tangible loyalty benefits
- Exceptional security for investors
- Fair and honest dealings
- Friendly, enjoyable service
- Local community support

As the Society has advanced and become markedly more profitable so it has given more and more benefits to members – thus highlighting the tangible returns from mutuality. In December 1997 the West Bromwich took the first step towards providing extra rate benefits to members. Returns for savers were increased by 0.25% gross per annum on all variable rate accounts, automatically increasing the competitiveness of the Society's already highly attractive savings portfolio. At the same time, the Society also reduced its variable mortgage base rate by 0.25%, at a time when banks were raising their mortgage rates.

An innovative Privileged Membership Scheme was also launched in 1997 to provide loyal members with an exclusive range of extra rate benefits, individual discounts and other preferential terms on a range of products and services. From 1 July 1999, the Privileged Mortgage Rate was 0.5% below the Society's standard rate for qualifying borrowers who had maintained their current mortgage product for five years or more. Similarly, the Privileged Membership Investment Account offered instant access to branch-based customers at a rate guaranteed to be no lower than 0.5% below Bank of the England base rate, with an extra 0.5% bonus if no withdrawals had been made during the account year. Through such initiatives the Society gave an extra £7 million in 1997 in rate benefits to members.

The 'virtuous circle' of mutuality was brought to the fore in 1999 by David Johnston, General Manager (Marketing). He recognised that no business could survive without making a profit or a surplus on its activities, but, significantly, mutual organisations like the West Bromwich were set apart from their public liability company counterparts by the way they chose to use their profits.

'As we increase mutuality benefits by enhancing savings and reducing mortgage rates for loyal customers, we increase our market share and achieve higher growth. This in turn lowers our operating costs and increases other income from a growing customer base. This leads to increased profits and allows us to pass on even more mutuality benefits.'

Defending Mutuality

Of course, every company needs to invest in its products, premises, technology and people, but plcs have to pay dividends to their shareholders with up to an estimated third of their profits swallowed up in this way. By contrast, mutuals do not have shareholders. Instead they have three groups of stakeholders – members, staff, and their local communities. Accordingly, whilst there must be investment in the business side, they can return much of their profit into giving members attractive interest rates and other benefits.

Regrettably, the principle of mutuality failed to affect those determined to make money for their own ends and the scourge of the carpetbaggers had not been fully deflected. In 1999 a resolution to convert to a bank was received from a small group of investors, led by a non-member who had become prominent in the campaign against mutuals. The Board unanimously agreed that conversion would not be in the long-term interest of the members, asserting that mutuals offered the best value. Importantly, the Board did not believe that the Society could survive as an independent plc and that there would be a clear risk to 'the jobs of 640 staff and our £20m support for the local community and economy. Branches would inevitably close and you, our members, would suffer.' Fortunately, the vast majority of the members of the Society were steadfast in their commitment to the idea of mutuality and voted not for demutualisation but for a mandate for mutuality.

To defend itself against the carpetbaggers, the West Bromwich had to raise minimum investment levels. Unfortunately, this 'excluded the very people we

Members at the Society's Annual General Meeting hear
of the Board's continued commitment to mutuality.

were set up to help. It even prevented us from launching certain new products.' To redress this and, at the same time, make the Society less appealing to carpetbaggers, from 1 October 1999 the Society asked investors to commit to 'charitable assignment' whereby they would hand over any windfall rights for five years to the Charities Aid Foundation. This move was directed at making 'the West Bromwich an unattractive target for speculators, whilst still allowing us to deliver the tangible benefits of mutuality to all our members'. The move also allowed the lowering of the minimum balance required on a number of accounts. Consequently children could join the Society with as little as £10 and many other accounts had a minimum balance of £100.

The commitment to mutuality was brought to the fore again in 2000 by the new chairman, Roger Dickens CBE. A Black Country man himself and former pupil of Tipton Grammar School, Roger went into accountancy when he was sixteen. Formerly UK deputy senior partner and a member of the UK, European and Asian Pacific Boards of KPMG, the global accountancy and management consultancy firm, Roger was a firm believer in the motto of 'one firm and one teamwork'. Under his leadership KPMG Midlands practice became the most profitable in the country. Vigorously attached to the ethos of public service, he had also been the President of the Birmingham Chamber of Commerce and Industry and was Deputy Lord Lieutenant of the West Midlands. In the Society's Annual Report for 2000 Roger asserted that 'building societies continue to enjoy a price advantage over their plc competitors. Our mutual status means that we do not have to pay dividends to outside shareholders and so we can provide extra value to our members through better interest rates and other benefits.' That year mutuality benefits to members rose to £10 million. Since then they have broken records year on year so that by the 31st March 2006 they had reached the impressive figure of £30million.

Mutuality is based upon respect, equality, co-operation and commitment and is a two-way process between the Society and members. Without the investment of members the Society could not succeed and it is essential that members not only receive benefits but also feel part of the Society to which they belong.

Members Matter

Members turn up to Annual General Meetings but the leadership of the Society also believed in increasing member participation further in the business. This saw the inauguration of the Members' Forum in 2002, allowing members a further say in their Society. The format of the Forums included a presentation by Andrew Messenger on the Society's performance and plans. Attended also by representatives of the Society's executive, these Forums allow members the opportunity to raise queries and issues in a direct face-to-face setting. The comments of members are taken seriously, as David Johnston, the Society's General Manager (Marketing), described: 'We lowered the minimum opening balance for our hugely popular Privileged Membership Investment Account from £500 to only £100. This was influenced by the feedback we were receiving from our customers, particularly in our heartland. Many qualified for and wanted the account but said the £500 limit precluded them.' By the summer of 2006, 10 Forums had been held at various venues, stretching across the whole of the Society's branch network.

Chief Executive, Andrew Messenger, takes questions during one of the Members' Forums, which were instigated to provide a further avenue for members to have a say in the Society.

Branching Out

Over the last decade or more many banks and building societies have closed down branches. In particular there are now few such facilities in more disadvantaged districts. This regrettable trend has exacerbated economic decline in many neighbourhoods and worsened social and economic deprivation. The West Bromwich has shunned such a socially negative approach that may add to short-term profitability but which, ultimately, creates long-term problems for less well-situated communities.

In 1999 the Society's affirmed its attachment to the branch network, especially within its West Midlands heartland. Telephone and post were becoming increasingly important in serving the needs of members, but branches represented the public face of the Society and enabled it to give members one-to-one help and advice at the point of sale through professionally qualified staff. This commitment to the branch network was apparent in the opening of new branches in Kings Heath, Birmingham, Tamworth and Telford. There were moves to prime sites, bigger premises such as at Coventry and Shrewsbury. Open-plan refurbishment took place at Walsall, West Bromwich, Erdington, Merry Hill, Stourbridge and Redditch.

Bev Bevan, legendary drummer with the world famous ELO,
hits the right note in opening the new branch in Kings Heath with
the Society's Angela Paskin and Stephen Karle.

The Society's Sutton branch is the toast of the town after being chosen by the readers for Sutton Coldfield Observer People's Choice Award.

The massive branch refurbishment programme was geared to providing customers with a relaxed and efficient environment.

This substantial outlay had the aim of creating an environment on a par with the very best in modern retailing, an environment where customers are able to discuss their financial needs in a relaxed and friendly atmosphere. The new layouts incorporated private interview areas and a children's play space. At the same time, security was increased with the introduction of secure lobbies and more use of CCTV.

Importantly, the investment in branches was balanced by work on the Principal Office. In 1999 that provided extra office space and meeting rooms to match the needs of an expanding business. Such improvements testified to the Society's commitment to the town of West Bromwich, rather than relocating to a larger site elsewhere – a powerful message in the Society's 150th year.

That significant anniversary was itself an opportunity for the Society to proudly proclaim its achievements over the course of its history and to trumpet its loyalty to mutuality and to its stakeholders – members, staff and community. Andrew Messenger encapsulated the mood:

'Our 150th Anniversary is, above all else, a celebration of our mutuality, and all that it involves. Throughout our long and distinguished history we have always sought to give our members value for money products and the very best service. We will continue to delight our customers through value added products and excellent, friendly service, delivered one to one by profession-ally qualifies staff in our branches, over the phone or through new electronic media such as e-mail and internet. We will continue to provide tangible and meaningful mutuality benefits. We will continue to invest in our staff, creating a multi-skilled, multi-talented workforce, wholly committed to meeting our customers' needs.'

Fittingly the climax of the 150th anniversary celebrations was held at the Black Country Living Museum in Dudley on 23 April 1999, both Saint George's Day and the actual day the Society was founded in West Bromwich. Given their staunch dedication to the ethic of working-class self help, to co-operation and to mutuality the Society's founders would have been proud of the progress made by their building society and by the Society's unshakeable belief in mutuality and the value of working with its members, staff and community.

Record Achievements

By 1997, the West Bromwich had largely recovered from the recession and had achieved everything it had set out to do some five years before. It had restored its underlying profitability and maintained its capital and financial strength. It had significantly reduced historic arrears through financial counselling and helping borrowers in difficulties. It had improved productivity and efficiency through better working practices and the development of technology. It had achieved controlled growth whilst improving the quality of assets through selective lending criteria and underwriting. And it had provided competitive investment and mortgage products to meet the prime financial needs of members.

Product innovation was essential and included the Pay Save scheme with leading local employers such as Sandwell Metropolitan Borough Council, LDV, Aeroquip and KPMG signing up to the Scheme. This deducted money direct from the payroll to the 'best buy' Regular Savings Account, encouraging people to develop the habit of saving.

The Society also launched affinity savings products with West Bromwich Albion, the Diocese of Lichfield and Warwickshire County Cricket Club, which offer attractive rates of interest together with financial support for these important local institutions.

1997 was a critical year for the Society. It had risen to become the twelfth largest society in the country and now possessed £2 billion worth of assets. From that strong and secure base the Society was poised to leap forward – and it did. In 1998 the West Bromwich enjoyed its best year ever. With an attractive range of Best Buy products and a high level of personal service, residential advances rose by 36% to £298 million. Significantly, this new business was of exceptional quality, with over 60% of advances made at, or below, 75% loan to value. Commercial lending was also up, by 40% to £38 million while assets passed the historic landmark of £2 billion.

Over 200 companies have signed up to the Society's PaySave Scheme,
which offers employees an easy and effective way to save regularly.
Staff at Red Mill Snack Foods taste the benefits of the scheme.

Providing members with long-term security, reserves accumulated to £150 million and in meeting customers' prime financial needs, other income grew to a record of £15 million a year. This resulted from close involvement with the Society's carefully chosen partners: General Accident for life assurance and regulated investments; Commercial Union (now Norwich Union) for house and contents insurance; London and Edinburgh (now part of Norwich Union), for accident, sickness and unemployment insurance; Capital Bank plc for personal loans; MBNA, for Visa credit cards; and Thomas Cook, for travel money.

The West Bromwich's desire to help out those in difficulty showed itself with the issue of arrears, which continued to drop significantly. This reflected several years of prudent growth, selective low-risk credit criteria and experience in underwriting. Importantly, as part of the Collections Department, there was an arrears team with the sensitivity and skill to act as financial counsellors, as well as arranging for external counsellors to visit a family facing money problems. As members of the Birmingham Arrears Liaison Group, the team produced a leaflet in various languages informing borrowers what to do and how to obtain help.

The key objective was to help customers rather than chase arrears. This meant a realistic plan for borrowers to make payments during their hard times. As ever with the West Bromwich, this approach to arrears was founded on strongly-held principles of wanting to help people. Accordingly, it embraced the writing of quality business; giving new residential mortgage customers of twelve months' free payment protection insurance; and permitting easier and more flexible direct debit payments. The result was astonishing. By 1998, the Society had reduced properties in possession from a peak of 566 to a mere 53.

Three years later the West Bromwich became the first lender in the country to actively help unemployed borrowers to find a job. With the desire to prevent borrowers falling into arrears, the Society welcomed constructive ways to help its customers. It resourced a team of consultants from specialist company Career Assist to advise unemployed borrowers on finding work. This groundbreaking scheme drew plaudits from the national media and led *The Times* in its City Comment to proclaim, 'it is laudable that the West Brom is at least trying to find a constructive way of helping its customers who find themselves in a mess. That would seem to embody the spirit of mutuality, a concept to which this society claims to be wedded.'

Embracing Technology

By the end of 1998 the West Bromwich boasted over 400,000 members and 43,000 mortgage customers served by forty-one branches, six Mortgage Bureaux and a Call Centre at the Principal Office for West Bromwich Direct, which administered savings accounts over the telephone. Launched in 1996, West Bromwich Direct was a telephone and postal service for investors. It quickly attracted more than 56,000 account holders and in excess of £500 million in savings, handling over 25,000 calls a month.

Manager (Business Analyst) Kath Arthur (centre) shows pupils from Whitesmore School the Society's IT facilities as part of their academic project.

To handle the dynamic growth of the Society, significant investment was made in IT systems to improve the efficiency and productivity of the whole organisation. This investment ensures the Society offers the most relevant and up-to-date services for customers. Investment was also made in reliable systems and technology to deliver product innovation, first class customer service and improved management information.

The Society has also developed a sophisticated customer database. This information is combined with Siebel, a market leading customer relationship system which tracks all customer contact with the Society. This allows information to be accessed by staff at any location, offering a quicker and more efficient service for customers.

OMNIA was replaced in 2001 by UFSS to provide improved flexibility and efficiency in processing both Investment and Mortgage accounts. UFSS was combined with a complex credit scoring system to provide instant information about the credit risk of customers applying for mortgages. Soon after, in 2002, a new system for branches was introduced – STAR – giving staff at branches complete information about customers visiting a branch.

Technology marched on and the Internet changed the way many customers wanted to do business. In response the Society developed two key Internet applications – a consumer web site and an Intermediary website. These award-winning systems provide information about the Society and its products, with the added advantage of enabling customers to apply, and get approval for a mortgage from the comfort of the customer's own home. The web sites are available 7 days a week 24 hours a day to provide a service whenever the Society's customers want it.

Building further on Internet technology, the Society introduced an internal internet to provide a communication network for all staff with information and help with work problems, all at the touch of a button.

West Bromwich will continue to explore how technology can provide benefits both to customers and the Society itself, making sure it remains a leader in products, service and efficiency.

Reaching New Heights

In 1998 the chairman was Ray Dickinson. Like all those who had held this high office in the Society, he was dedicated to public service. Active in charity work, he had been Managing Director of what was then one of West Bromwich's largest companies, security printers Kenrick and Jefferson. In his report he emphasised that despite 'difficult trading conditions and intense competition, your Society has performed consistently well. Last year was certainly no exception. Once again, we produced good results in both the mortgage and savings markets, with other income continuing to make a growing and important contribution.'

The Chairman went on to draw attention to an 'outstanding team of people' led by Andrew Messenger, who had taken the Society 'to new heights. His con-

Ray Dickinson, Chairman of the West Bromwich from 1998 to 1999.

tribution, dedication and vision have enabled us to put in place a strong financial base to take our business forward into the 21st century.' Importantly, Andrew had been supported 'by an extremely capable and experienced senior management team, and by talented and committed staff at all levels and throughout all areas of the Society'. The great strides made by the Society were affirmed by the award of the Richardson Trophy given by Sandwell and Dudley Chamber of Commerce for outstanding business performance by Black Country firms. Ian Brough, the Chamber's chief executive, was 'delighted that the Society, a mutual organisation, has outstripped the plcs to win this award.'

Benefiting both from dynamic and intelligent leadership and a motivated and loyal staff, the West Bromwich rose to amazing heights in the new millennium.

In 2001, *People*, the Society's magazine for customers, proudly declared that 'the West Brom goes from strength to strength. Annual results published at the beginning of June show that it has been a record year for the Society, confirming our position as one of the top ten building societies in the UK'. Boasting 450,000 members the Society's assets now stood at £3.3 billion, up almost 19% on the previous year. This enormous figure represented a phenomenal growth rate of 88% over the previous five years. Lending was also at an all-time high, up 39% to £727 million. Another record was set for gross other income, up by 23% to £25.5 million. This exceptional performance was, according to Andrew Messenger, 'among the best in the building society sector and the accumulation of the huge efforts we have made over the past few years. And we will continue to improve our

Chief Executive, Andrew Messenger, displays the trophies for Best Large Company and Best Equal Opportunities Employer, a remarkable double-winning performance by the Society at the 2001 Midlands Excellence Awards.

efficiency and productivity even further, so that we can continue to grow, thrive and share our ongoing success with our members, staff and communities.'

That promise has been made good. Year on year the West Bromwich has smashed record after record. In 2002, the Society's Chairman, Roger Dickens, proclaimed that 'the past twelve months have been the most successful in the Society's long and distinguished history'. Growth of 12.4% had taken assets to £3.7 billion. As in previous years under Andrew Messenger's stirring leadership, the Society was almost a permanent fixture in the 'best buy' mortgage and savings table – and, as ever, the Chief Executive extolled the virtues of mutuality:

'we have probably delivered the best results in the building society sector, but this has only been possible because of our people – members, staff and community. It makes me enormously proud to be part of this fantastic team – I hope we make members feel proud to be part of that team, too.'

That year the West Bromwich was placed fifth among the top 35 mortgage lenders in the United Kingdom by *Moneyfacts*, the country's leading independent authority on mortgage and savings rates. The Society was also delighted when Andrew Messenger received the Leadership Award at the Mortgage Finance Gazette Awards. This is given to individuals who are regarded as stars in their own field. In Andrew's case the panel of adjudicators cited his leadership skills in transforming the West Bromwich over the previous decade, enabling it to overcome the challenges facing it as the Society became one of the most successful mutual building societies in the UK.

Centre of Excellence

Neither Andrew, his Board, his senior management team, nor the staff of the West Bromwich took their success for granted. Each year's record results were greeted with the resolve to work tirelessly to grow, thrive and share that success with the Society's members.

The launch of a new £2 million Contact Centre in 2002 exemplified this assertive approach. Based at the Society's Principal Office it was able to handle half a million calls a year, ranging from enquiries about mortgages and investments to questions about buildings insurance. Equipped with new technology, the details relating to a customer were instantly available, saving the customer from having to repeat the query as so often happens with large-scale organisations. Imbued with a 'one-stop one-solution' approach the Contact Centre staff were highly trained in technical and personal skills.

Heather Foote, manager of the Centre, was thrilled at the new initiative as 'we aspire to provide a service that meets modern day demands while retaining the traditional human touch. In doing so the Contact Centre will become a centre of excellence and standard-bearer in the field.' With 120 staff, the Contact Centre rapidly made its mark and was named top Contact Centre at

Jacqui Smith MP, Government Minister for Diversity, officially opens the Society's state-of-the-art Contact Centre with Chairman, Roger Dickens.

The Society's commitment to customer care is epitomised by Paula Dajczak, who was named Contact Centre Professional of the Year, beating thousands of contenders across the country.

the Mittel International Call Centre Awards in 2004. The quality of staff was epitomised by Paula Dajczak, who took the prized honour of Contact Centre Professional of the Year at the National Customer Service awards (2003). This was a magnificent achievement given competition from more than a million people working in call centres around the United Kingdom. From the perspective of the Society's expansion, the Contact Centre was a keystone in the West Bromwich's capacity to extend its reach to all corners of the UK, allowing the Society to attain a truly national presence.

Increase in Intermediary Business

This growth in custom had also been enhanced by the development of the Intermediary Services Division. Dealing with estate agents, insurance companies and independent financial advisers, who recommend customers to the West Bromwich, such 'introducers' are attracted to the Society by its values of integrity, credibility and flexibility. Paul Cuthbert, then manager at Nottingham, made this clear: 'it is about how you present yourself to other businesses. In that sense, you are selling your personality first. Once people are convinced by you and your integrity, it is then much easier to meet their financial needs.'

The growing importance of the Intermediary Services Division to the expansion of the Society was expressed by figures for 2005/06 when it accounted for £969 million, almost 76% of all residential lending. The increasing impact of this section of the business saw it assume the distinct identity of West Brom for Intermediaries in 2006, which highlighted the specialist nature and enormous contribution of this arm of the Society. Aided by its own highly-regarded website, www.westbromforintermediaries.co.uk Paul Marland, assistant general manager for Intermediary Sales, stated: 'This new brand will enable us to up our performance to yet higher levels, resulting ultimately in increased benefits for the overall West Brom Group and its stated mission of becoming the best performing building society in the country."

Going From Strength to Strength

In 2003 the West Bromwich announced one of the best results in the building society sector. At 15% growth was amongst the highest in the industry, and for the first time the Society broke through the £4 billion barrier in assets. Lending was up an astonishing 39% to £1 billion whilst pre-tax profits leaped by 14% to £27.5 million. In surpassing the previous year's record results so spectacularly the West Bromwich won the Moneyfacts Award for Best Fixed Rate Mortgage Provider. In addition *Your Mortgage* and the *Investors Association* highlighted the Society's constant capacity to provide value-for-money 'Best Buy' products.

These national awards were matched by a major accolade in its heartland. At the Best of Black Country Awards, sponsored by the *Express and Star,* the West

The Board has high calibre directors with the expertise and experience to help guide the Society's strategic direction.

Bromwich was awarded a special prize for the way 'it has transformed itself so dramatically in recent years by the use of best practice in business, and within the community, that the judges felt it stands apart in a class of its own'. In all the Society gained fifteen awards and numerous commendations, encouraging the Society's Chairman, Roger Dickens, to proclaim that 'it is a tremendous record of achievement, bringing a deep sense of pride to all those associated with the West Bromwich Building Society. It is a fabulous testimony to the way we treat our customers, our staff and the people who live and work in the communities we serve. What these awards ultimately signify is that we really do practice what we preach.'

For the seventh year running, in 2004 the West Bromwich excelled itself with record after record from the previous year broken. Assets now exceeded £5 billion and the following year witnessed more financial records being broken. In 2005, assets surged to £6 billion and pre-tax profits to £33.7 million. Commenting on yet another year of outstanding performance by the West Bromwich, Andrew Messenger outlined some of the reasons for the Society's tremendous achievements. These were:

'a clear strategy and commitment to customer value and service in a year characterised by fierce competition, increased regulation and uncertainty over markets and business conditions. Our future focus will be on delivering profitable growth, increasing our financial strength, and offering exceptional value, advice and service to members. Our strategy of maximising returns from subsidiary businesses, which complements the Society's operation and provides access to new markets, will continue at a pace.'

Chairman, Roger Dickens, with a selection of awards won by the Society in recent years, covering customer service, value-for-money products, staff welfare, diversity and community involvement.

As Andrew went on to say:

'Our success in meeting members needs will be seen not only through financial achievements, but also by measuring customer and employee satisfaction. We will do more to ensure all our employees continue to develop their knowledge and skills to care for and advise members and that they are equipped to carry greater responsibility for meeting customers' ongoing needs. This will be supported by their unceasing commitment to serving members.'

The Success of Subsidiaries

A major part of the 2005 success story was related to the three wholly-owned subsidiaries of the Society. In fact 40% of the pre-tax profit of £33.7 million was attributable to the West Bromwich Mortgage Company, West Bromwich Homes, and West Bromwich Commercial.

The West Bromwich Mortgage Company had celebrated ten years of operation and was very much a success story in its own right. With over £750 million in assets and 9,000 mortgage customers, it was the equivalent to the 22nd largest building society in the country. Its brief is to purchase mortgage assets and then offer borrowers a full mortgage service. Up to 2005 it had bought twenty mortgage portfolios, including major purchases from AXA, GMAC, Kensington, and the Wesleyan. David Mackay, Managing Director of the company, was confident that with its expertise and experience 'the future will reap further rewards both for the Company and the Society, increasing the profit we make for the ultimate benefit of the member'.

West Bromwich Homes was established in 1997 and has now widened its operation to the stage where, in 2006, it possesses a portfolio of over 800 properties. Tenants tended to be families, people moving to a new job especially in the public sector, and first-time buyers struggling to gain a foothold on the housing ladder. Stephen Potter, its Managing Director, was certain that 'we are meeting genuine housing need with high-quality accommodation, a purpose that echoes the Society's founding ethos.'

Another sector of the Society which has made a huge impact on the record breaking run of the West Bromwich is another of the Society's subsidiaries, West Bromwich Commercial. The company provides mortgage finance to companies and organisations so that they may buy offices, shops, government buildings and other commercial property. In 1996 the team loaned £30 million, but by the end

David Mackay, Managing Director, West Bromwich Mortgage Company,
celebrates the 10th anniversary of this burgeoning subsidiary with
(left) Joanne Trickett and Sarah Wilkinson.

Rob Clifford, Managing Director of Mortgage Force, the Society's most recently acquired subsidiary, receives the Mortgage Strategy Award from media figure, Clive Anderson (left) and Michael Bolton, the Award's sponsor.

of the financial year 2005/06 that figure had soared to £476 million, a truly superb effort. Mike Nixon, Managing Director of Commercial Lending, was aware that 'as with residential properties, the customer is still looking for the same thing – a mortgage from a reputable and reliable lender at an attractive rate. And as our recent record shows, the West Brom fits that description perfectly.'

This commercial lending covers the whole country, including the south east of England, and custom is often obtained through intermediaries. As Mark Pagett, Manager with West Bromwich Commercial, asserted, these intermediaries deal with 'a superb team of very experienced and extremely able individuals with a background in corporate banking, which gives us the confidence to ensure this section of the business prospers.'

The success of the subsidiary businesses was bolstered by Mortgage Force, which was acquired by the Society in 2005. An award-winning company that was the country's leading franchised mortgage broker, it is anticipated that Mortgage Force will open up new markets and enhance the Society's plans for growth.

The Pursuit of Progress

In the global world of finance, international as much as national economic trends can make or break institutions that do not adapt, innovate and look ahead. Whilst affirming its traditional values the West Bromwich is determined that it shall be flexible and pioneering and willing to establish partnerships with other organisations for the good of its members. To these ends, in March 2006, the Society announced that it would be offering mortgage protection products to its customers through a new partner, Friends Provident, one of the United Kingdom's leading financial services groups. Friends Provident was chosen because it was a highly respected and trusted company with a reputation for quality service and award-winning products.

The partnership with a major financial institution was balanced by the responsibility the Society felt towards smaller organisations that were working at the grass roots level. At the beginning of 2006, it backed the re-launch of the Sandwell 6 Towns Credit Union at 382 High Street, West Bromwich. The Union's remit clearly chimed with the Society's own values by offering an invaluable service to local people on low incomes, who were often financially marginalised. Loraine Furness, Mortgage and Credit Services Manager at the West Bromwich Building Society, explained: 'It is vital that members of the public are given as much professional information and advice about how to budget and cope with the demands that borrowing in particular can bring. Our major concern is that, in moments of desperation, people turn to loan sharks and unauthorised money lenders for a quick-fix. This can lead to crippling and scandalous rates of interest and threats of violence when the person is unable to repay the debt.' The Sandwell 6 Towns Credit Union plays a major role in enabling people to avoid this terrible trap by teaching and assisting them to save.

In its link with the Sandwell 6 Towns Credit Union the West Bromwich Building Society brings to the fore the principle that its commitment to caring for members is matched by a commitment to the wider community. Those commitments are inextricably bound up with each other and with the ethos of the Society. Together they have been at the heart of the business and financial success of the West Bromwich.

Community Support

Propelling the Society's name into the community was vital in the spectacular financial growth of the Society. From its beginning the Society has played an active role in, and supported, the community from which it has grown. One of the key initiatives in raising the Society's name profile came with its sponsorship of West Bromwich Albion Football Club. The connection between the two most important bodies that carry the name of the town began in the 1960s when the Society advertised at the Hawthorns, the Albion's ground, with the slogan 'Money Well Saved with the West Bromwich Building Society'. Then, following the 1968 FA Cup Final triumph, goal-scoring hero Jeff Astle featured on posters in the Society's branches to attract business.

Strong community and financial links between the two institutions were re-established in 1992 when the Society sponsored the Albion's family stand. In May 1997 the tie was reinforced when a sponsorship deal was signed whereby the Baggies carried the logo of the West Bromwich Building Society on their shirts. According to Tony Dubberley, General Manager (Sales), both the Society

Together with West Bromwich Albion, Chairman, Jeremy Peace (right), and TV sports presenter, Gary Newbon, Chief Executive, Andrew Messenger, proudly displays the Society's logo as part of the shirt sponsorship deal with the football club.

and the club 'have a great tradition serving the town and are very proud of our roots here in the Black Country'.

During the mid-1990s an Albion Premier Saver Account was launched – the first of its kind in the country. This gave fans instant access to savings and very attractive interest rates, as well as offering incentives such as cheaper season tickets for the family stand. The West Bromwich agreed to make an annual cash payment to the Albion equal to 1% gross interest on the total average balance in the account over a twelve-month period. It was a tremendous success and, in 2005, had drawn in over 10,000 fans, earning in aggregate more than £1.2 million for the Baggies since its launch.

By 2006 there were several affinity schemes, incorporating the major football clubs in the West Midlands – West Bromwich Albion, Aston Villa, Birmingham City and Coventry City. But the schemes also spread out to net the likes of Leicester City in the East Midlands and, at the humbler end of the football hierarchy, Kidderminster Harriers, Shrewsbury Town, and Chester City where income from the affinity schemes brought real benefits to an often precarious existence for these clubs.

It could be said that sporting institutions were a prevalent theme in the affinity accounts. As well as football, the West Bromwich also opened the Century

Rob Williams, the Society's Senior Manager for Operations (centre) teams up with Walsall's manager, Colin Lee, and (right) Martin O'Connor to promote the Saddlers Super Saver Account.

*The Society's Stephen Karle (second right)
gets the new shirt sponsorship off the mark
with (from left) Jim Troughton, Colin Povey,
Chief Executive of Warwickshire County
Cricket Club, and Dougie Brown.*

Savers Account with one of the country's leading cricket counties, Warwickshire, in 1997. This has certainly proved a productive partnership with a total of more than £300,000 raised for the club by the beginning of 2006. In addition, 2005 also saw the West Bromwich become shirt sponsors of the county, and the Society's name could be seen emblazoned around the famous Edgbaston ground during the epic nerve-tingling Ashes encounter between England and Australia that summer.

However, while sport clearly dominated the range of affinity accounts, the West Bromwich was also determined to embrace other kinds of organisations with roots in their local communities. For instance, the Severn Valley Railway, a not-for-profit organisation that relies on volunteers and with over 30,000 supporters, also gained from linking up with the West Bromwich on an affinity scheme. Similarly, with the Diocese of Lichfield where a Community Account was set up in 1997. This fund, which was later administered through the Church Urban Fund and Mercian Trust, promoted urban regeneration and a variety of community projects across the region, all with a visible humanitarian vocation. This encompassed projects for homeless people, centres for improving the skills and aptitudes of unemployed individuals, educational initiatives for young people excluded from school, and provision for the victims of domestic violence.

The Diocese of Lichfield Church Fund has brought enormous benefits for many disadvantaged social groups. Here, Roger Smith, the Society's Group Development Director, presents a contribution to the retiring Bishop of Lichfield, Right Reverend Keith Sutton (centre), and the Archdeacon of Walsall, the Venerable Tony Sadler.

Investing in Youth

Helping children and youngsters is indeed a longstanding aim of the West Bromwich. The NSPCC Full Stop campaign, which seeks to end cruelty to children within a generation, is a life-changing body that has received significant funds from the West Bromwich. In 2000 the Society pledged to raise £50,000 for the campaign. That sum was reached in just over a year, thanks to the wholehearted dedication of staff, who put on a wide range of creative and enthusiastic events.

On another front, the Society's link-up with West Bromwich Albion saw the launch of the Albion Community Programme in 1995. Using football as a device

The Society's General Manager (Sales) Tony Dubberley, toasts the 10th anniversary of the Albion Community Programme with Albion Chairman, Jeremy Peace (sitting), and Programme Director, Fraser Foster (left).

for tackling the educational and recreational needs of young people, the Programme proved a real winner, helping young people improve their academic performance, including a special project for more disaffected adolescents. By the time the Programme had celebrated its 10th anniversary in 2005, over 500,000 had taken part in the programme.

That concern with helping young people realise their potential was also manifested in the Society's sponsorship of the Sandwell Duke of Edinburgh Awards Scheme Committee, commencing in 1992. Working with Sandwell Metropolitan Borough Council, the Society helped to train some 100 Duke of Edinburgh Award leaders in a seven-year period, resulting in more than 230 young people gaining awards. In 2001, when over 500 young people were involved in many different activities in the scheme, HRH Prince Edward, the Earl of Wessex, visited the Society's Principal Office to meet youngsters, who had successfully participated in the Scheme.

The Society's Chairman, Roger Dickens, presents HRH Prince Edward, the Earl of Wessex, with a commemorative portrait of the West Bromwich Mural during the royal visit to mark the Duke of Edinburgh Award Scheme.

The Society's Paul Turner (second left) shows his backing for the Outward Bound initiative with Alan Crisp, Course Instructor, Mick Kearns of Walsall FC and John Price, Walsall Education Business Partnership, with (front) Sam Bennett.

Again, as a further example of this commitment to children and young people, the Society gave a £10,000 bursary in 1999 to help teenagers from socially deprived areas in the West Midlands spend a week with the Outward Bound Trust in mid-Wales. Several of the youngsters recollected it as 'as a once-in-a-lifetime experience'. They were able to go canoeing, mountaineering, rafting, abseiling and gorge sailing, learning much about themselves as individuals and about the attributes of team work and co-operation. This has been repeated every year since and remains an important feature in the West Bromwich's community calendar.

Caring for Others

Fundraising initiatives by staff are myriad and imaginative – and simply too numerous to list in detail. Some of the highlights included: a team ran in the London Marathon, raising £15,000 for Shelter's work with children whose lives are overshadowed by homelessness or bad accommodation; the renowned BBC Children in Need Appeal is eagerly supported across the branch network, as exemplified by staff at the West Smethwick branch, who collected over

Society staff get ready to run the London Marathon for Shelter.

£700 by transforming their premises into a mini-Bollywood through dressing up in costumes, decking the branch with giant film posters and playing music from well-known Bollywood films; Macmillan Cancer Relief gained from a series of coffee mornings held in branches; a group for people in retirement, providing much-needed social contact and stimulation for many isolated older people, was supported by the West Bromwich; staff undertook a parachute jump for a children's hospital in Swindon; the Society sponsored the world famous and record-breaking Santa Run in Newtown, which raises a huge sum each year for Dial-a-Ride, the town's mobility scheme that does so much to improve the quality of life for older and disabled members of the community; and, as an inspiring indicator of the West Bromwich's compassion, the Society, aided by the altruistic impetus of staff, donated over £60,000 towards alleviating the suffering caused by the harrowing Tsunami disaster, which struck at the beginning of 2005.

In all, countless organisations and projects have benefited from the generosity and goodwill of the West Bromwich and its staff, initiatives that have covered the needs of children and young people, educational opportunities, older people, disability, mental health, poverty and social disadvantage.

The Society's West Smethwick branch captures the magic of Bollywood for the BBC's Children in Need Appeal.

Newton becomes a sea of red for the world record-breaking Santa Run,
which the Society has sponsored from its beginning in 2001.

Staff at the Great Barr branch take part in a special fund-raising day
for the emergency appeal following the Tsunami disaster.

Victoria Platt's car receives a sparkling wash from the colleagues
Andy Wood, Lisa McHugh and Ian Ponter as part of a fund-raising
event for the British Heart Foundation.

Each year the Society pledges to raise a sizeable sum for a selected charity. As well as the NSPCC, other nominated charities have benefited from the enthusiastic kindness of staff, notably Cancer Research UK, Help the Aged, the British Heart Foundation and, in 2006, Birmingham Children's Hospital, which has earned a worldwide, as well as national, reputation for its care and treatment of children. Once more, the staff's wonderful ingenuity and humanity have been abundantly apparent with a series of fund-raising activities for these vital causes.

The Campaigning Society

In the last few years the community activities of the Society have broadened to include campaigns with a wider national repercussion and not solely confined to members or customers of the West Bromwich. Extolling the original aim of the founders of the Society to expand home ownership, the West Bromwich launched a Raise the Roof campaign in 2005. Motivated by a determination to make it easier for people on low incomes and first-time buyers to purchase their own homes, Andrew Messenger issued a battle cry to the nation to join him in his crusade to persuade Chancellor Gordon Brown to "Raise the Roof" on Stamp Duty in his next budget. He explained:

> 'At present, the first band of Stamp Duty is charged at 1% on properties over £60,000. You will appreciate that, because of the rise in house prices in recent years, virtually every property now qualifies for Stamp Duty. I believe this is utterly wrong and unfair. I believe it is possible that, with sufficient pressure from the general public, we can persuade the Chancellor to raise the threshold at which Stamp Duty is charged from the current £60,000 to £150,000. This would be in line with current house price inflation. As house prices rise so too does the percentage of people who qualify to pay stamp duty, regardless of their income.'

Banners were unveiled outside the Principal office of the West Bromwich, publicising support for the campaign with a website address www.westbrom.co.uk. Petitions for customers and staff to sign were made available in each of the Society's 48 branches and were then made available to other building societies, financial service providers and the public across the whole of the UK as the campaign gained in strength from backing by influential members of the national media.

On Thursday 3 March 2005 Andrew Messenger, in the company of other building society chiefs, presented the Chancellor with a petition of over 23,000 signatures. Intent on influencing the Government in an election year, the campaigners succeeded. In his 2005 Budget the Chancellor raised the Stamp Duty threshold to £120,000. Even though the figure did not reach the hoped for £150,000, Andrew Messenger praised Gordon Brown on behalf of the estimated 373,000 first-time buyers nationally who will benefit from this measure.

*Chief Executive, Andrew Messenger, launches the Society's 'Raise the Roof'
campaign to raise the threshold on Stamp Duty.*

*The Society, backed by other organisations, takes its Stamp Duty petition
to the Chancellor in Downing Street.*

Within weeks the West Bromwich was reacting swiftly to the disastrous collapse of MG Rover at Longbridge. More than 5,000 people lost their jobs while others in supply firms were also hit hard by this devastating event. This bad news came at a time when manufacturing was already haemorrhaging jobs in the West Midlands. The West Bromwich quickly offered financial counselling, referral to specialist job agencies, and specific product assistance such as interest only payments to workers who had mortgages with the Society.

Later in the year, the West Bromwich decided to take up the cause of people in retirement, a concern sparked by the darkening 'pensions crisis', which estimated a £27 billion shortfall in savings for retirement. Entitled 'Make Retirement Work For All' the campaign called on the Chancellor to take radical action in his budget to help people in retirement, savers, and first-time buyers. As Andrew Messenger affirmed, 'the West Bromwich aims to look after people so that they can look forward with confidence to a longer life by helping make their retirement financially trouble free. That is why our campaign is so important.'

Armed with a set of compelling figures, Andrew Messenger asserted that pensioners faced a precarious future; that 50% of UK households have less than £1,500 in savings and 28% (7 million households) have no savings at all; and the number of first time buyers has reached its lowest level for 25 years. An estimated 320,000 buyers stepped onto the housing ladder in 2005, the lowest since

Chief Executive, Andrew Messenger, joins the Mayor of Birmingham,
TV presenter, Gary Newbon, and members of a local pensioners' group to get the
'Make Retirement Work For All' campaign on track.

1980; moreover, 50% of first time buyers had insufficient savings to pay a deposit to buy their first home. Many first-time buyers also had escalating and dangerously high personal debt.

This daunting picture promised little sign of improvement and required targeted and innovative measures. As an immediate and necessary response, Andrew Messenger urged the Chancellor to introduce a set of wide-ranging measures. To encourage saving specifically for retirement he looked for an increase in the Cash ISA limit to £7,000 for the over fifties and stop taxing savings up to a £10,000 balance.

To help people to help themselves he exhorted the Chancellor not to penalise homeowners who wished to unlock the value built up in their property to provide much-needed income in retirement and to exclude income from lifetime mortgages in means tested benefits. These measures needed to be backed by a simplification of the Benefits System. In particular the campaign called for the introduction of a single, simple, streamlined application form for all retirement benefits from a single government agency.

The West Bromwich did not just demand. It acted decisively itself. Figures from pensioner charity organisations showed that as many as 700,000 pensioners may not have been getting the benefits that they were entitled to. Under the Society's 'Make Retirement Work For All' campaign, the West Bromwich introduced a free service to help pensioners claim those benefits through a specially developed computer programme. Available in four branches, as part of a pilot

Chief Executive, Andrew Messenger, outlines the Society's
campaign at one of the Retirement Roadshows.

initiative, it allowed retired customers to have a quick assessment of their bene-fits entitlements and to obtain relevant contact numbers for benefits agencies.

This campaign has been accompanied by Pensioner Roadshows as part of the Society's desire to take the campaign message into the wider community. Together with advice from Help the Aged, pensioners could hear from Andrew Messenger and various Society managers expert in the issues affecting people in retirement, such as Inheritance Tax Planning, estate planning, annuity broking, pension consolidation, and the Society's special Oak Account for the over 60s that offered a competitive rate of 4.0%. Indeed, as more and more people have found themselves ensnared in the inheritance tax trap, the West Bromwich has joined up with the local media to produce a special booklet and financial semi-nars to offer assistance to people to minimise the impact of this tax.

In tandem with this programme the West Bromwich offered savers its Paysave Schemes, Affinity Accounts, and Privileged Membership Investment Account. Finally, the Society's First-time Buyer Proposition aimed to improve the position of people struggling to get a foothold on the property ladder. This included a low start repayment with interest only for the first five years; a pro-fessional mortgage allowing key workers such as doctors, teachers, nurses to borrow more; lending in partnership with Housing Associations; an affordabili-ty assessment to increase to a multiple of five times income; 100% shared own-ership schemes; and a facility to offset a mortgage with family contributions so as to reduce the mortgage term or monthly repayments.

With the decline of manufacturing industry in the West Midlands and the loss of socially responsible companies, such as Rubery Owen and Lucas, the West Bromwich Building Society has taken over the mantle of leadership by example. Its very existence is predicated upon the principles of putting something back into the community, of empowering people to achieve their ambitions, and of working with the vulnerable and marginalised. In an era when conviction politics have declined and when less privileged people see themselves as marginalised then the campaigning role of the West Bromwich has become vital in advocating their cause.

People Make the Difference

As Andrew Messenger asserted in 1998 'we are committed to investing in our people. They are, and will remain, central to our success. Their enthusiasm, camaraderie and team spirit inspire us all'. He went on to stress that 'the provi-sion of financial services is, and will remain, a people business. People have always been at the heart of everything we do. They have provided the cause, the motivation and the customer service. Individually and collectively they have been the driving force behind our long history and success. And the proof of our suc-cess is there for all see in the financial reports and in our increasing market share.'

The Society's investment in people and commitment to quality service have been recognised externally with a string of awards. In 1998 the Society won first

prize in the Company of the Year Awards 500 to 1,000 employees category for
the Wales and Midlands region. It also received a commendation in the West
Midlands Regional Training Awards sponsored by the West Midlands Regional
Training and Enterprise Councils. This body stated that the award was 'a spectacular reinforcement of West Bromwich's position as one of the region's leading building societies'.

This belief in investing in people was vividly demonstrated when the Society
opened a training suite in 1997, allowing staff at all levels to develop and expand
their skills and educational opportunities.

Pertinently, the number of staff who were either studying for or who had professional qualifications had shot up from 19% to 67% in the previous five years.
This impressive rise was part of the West Bromwich's Our People Strategy 2004.
Paul Turner, General Manager (people development), expounded the thinking
behind this approach:

'By equipping our staff with the relevant skills, knowledge and behaviours
they'll be able to deliver a real competitive advantage while also achieving
their full potential. Our strategy embraces all aspects of people development
but one area where we have seen quite spectacular results is training and
development.'

*Two of the Society's
long-serving staff,
Madeline Page, and
(right) Pauline Green
participate in a special
fund-raising day for
Cancer Research UK.*

Talent and training are key factors in the success of the West Bromwich. The Society believes in taking talented individuals and offering them a level of training and support which ensures such talent is harnessed – for the benefit of the individual and customers. A key facility is the Staff Training and Development Unit where staff can gain the skills and knowledge to help maintain the West Bromwich's remarkable progress.

The striking training success of the West Bromwich is equalled by that of the People Development Team. Occupying a prime position within the Society it encourages staff to do their best and assists with community activities. In 2001 this team received the Excellence in Community Involvement trophy at the Human Resources Excellence Awards. The next year Paul Turner set up a Culture Change Group (CCG) which sought to develop a culture that supports West Bromwich Building Society values whilst enabling the delivery of business targets.

In 2003 the People Support team received the Managing Health At Work prize in the Personnel Today awards. Then, in 2004, the People team surpassed itself at the Personnel Today awards by taking the title of Best HR Strategy and Overall Awards Winner. Paul Turner, General Manager for People, elucidated the vision of his team 'which is to make sure everyone feels valued and has the opportunity to make a significant contribution to the business and to their own personal development.' That belief in nourishing and appreciating staff found national acknowledgement when the Society won the award for Employee Satisfaction at the UK Business Excellence Awards in 2005 – a genuine register of how the West Bromwich really cares about its staff.

The People Team celebrate taking the title of
Overall Winner at the Personnel Today awards.

A Beacon of Diversity

'Diversity' is the watchword throughout the Society's workplace policies. The West Bromwich welcomes individuals with ability, potential and dedication, whatever their ethnicity, gender, or disability. This is reflected in the various groups at the West Bromwich set up to advise and monitor the Society's progress on diversity. 'Women at West Brom' has already attained an admirable reputation since its formation in 2002. Having a concern to highlight issues affecting

Representatives of Women at West Brom present Christmas gifts to staff of Sandwell Women's Aid, who cater for women and children suffering domestic violence and abuse.

women, both within and outside the the Society, Women at West Brom has been instrumental in the introduction of relevant policies to accommodate the particular pressures of parents with children, such as flexible and term-time working. In addition, the group has an awareness of the wider social and personal predicaments afflicting many women, as evidenced by its support for the work of Sandwell Women's Aid with victims of domestic violence.

Stephen Karle, who becomes the Chief Executive of the West Bromwich in October 2006, was an influential leader in promoting the Society's commitment to diversity, championing the Society's emulation of the Business Excellence model.[2]

This commitment to diversity was revealed at every level within the Society. For instance, the West Bromwich bolstered its policy of actively encouraging and supporting female staff by appointing Lesley James CBE to its Board room in 2001. Previously Director of Human Resources at Tesco and a holder of senior positions in a number of leading companies, Lesley was joined the following year by Sue Battle. Then Chief Executive of the Birmingham, Chamber of Commerce, Sue has been a prominent figure not only in business but also in promoting the economic well being of the West Midlands.

Staff enthusiastically support the Society's efforts on behalf of its nominated charity for 2004, Help the Aged, which does so much to benefit the older members of the community.

Under the flag of diversity, the Society also convenes a 'Disability Steering Group', which works to improve the employment prospects and service adjustments for people with disabilities. The proportion of employees with a disability increased by 40% during 2004 alone. The Society has also been actively involved with Rehab UK, an organisation that supports individuals who have experienced severe illnesses, by providing work experience as part of the return to work process. Ageism is another prejudice the West Bromwich has sought to tackle with branch roadshows in liaison with Saga FM as part of an awareness programme on age discrimination. The Society's 'Make Retirement Work For All' campaign is also an emphatic example of the West Bromwich's practical advocacy for older people.

The West Bromwich's branch network is predominantly located in the West Midlands, one of the most ethnically diverse regions in the country. The Society fervently believes such diversity should be mirrored in the composition of its staff. Accordingly, over 18% of the Society's staff in 2006 had an ethnic minority background, a figure above the national average. At Board level, too, the Society was delighted to have the services of Ambar Paul, chairman and chief executive of Caparo Industries plc. In 2004 Ugandan-born Bharat Shah joined the Board. Bharat had headed Kodak's consumer business operations in Europe, Asia and the Middle East. This background gave him a keen sensitivity of the varying needs of a diverse, multi-cultural workforce and community, echoing the Society's own commitment on race and diversity.

The importance of the Society's ethnic profile meant it was able to offer a service to ethnic minority customers that was culturally sensitive, especially in areas with a high ethnic minority population. This meant speaking the language of customers, producing bi-lingual promotional material, having an understanding of cultural customs and, as part of the Society's commitment to the community, celebrating major festivals, such as Diwali and Eid.

This awareness precipitated a number of imaginative marketing initiatives, in particular partnerships with the two most popular Asian radio stations in the Midlands – Radio XL in Birmingham and Sabras Sound in Leicester. Ethnic minority staff from the West Bromwich appeared on special phone-in shows, offering information in appropriate languages on such issues as mortgages, savings, inheritance tax, and community involvement. In 2006, the West Bromwich inaugurated a similar relationship with New Style Radio in Birmingham, which catered for the African Caribbean population in the area.

As a forceful emblem of its commitment to racial equality, the Society has been an exemplary member of Race for Opportunity (RfO), a campaign of Business in the Community. RfO is a national programme that seeks to promote the interests of ethnic minorities while delivering real benefits to each and every organisation that chooses to engage positively with this vital and growing sector of our community. Andrew Messenger, himself Chair of Race for Opportunity in the West Midlands, explained the need to participate in RfO:

The Society's Saroj Williams with Radio XL presenter, Arun Sharma,
as part of the Society on-air advice programmes.

'We see RfO as part of our social responsibility and also as an opportunity to increase our business. The campaign aims to bring organisations and ethnic minority communities closer together to work to their mutual advantage. Given our commitment to mutuality and the fact that we have a high proportion of ethnic minorities among our staff and in our local communities, it is our ethical and economic duty to be involved.'

In 2006 the Society came 2nd overall nationally and was named top regionally based organisation in the Race for Opportunity Benchmarking Report – the most authoritative study on how well organisations in the public and private sectors are performing on race. In all, over 110 organisations took part in the benchmarking exercise, including the likes of Jaguar, HSBC, Severn Trent, Army, CadburyTreborBassett and the BBC, illuminating how the Society has become a beacon of excellence in this field.

The Society's shining example on diversity brought additional accolades. In 2001, the Society was named Equal Opportunities Employer of the Year at the Midlands Excellence Awards, which followed immediately in the footsteps of the award for Best Large Company – a remarkable double triumph that was the envy of many. And the litany of achievement did not end there. At the Financial Services Innovation Awards of 2002 the Society picked up the prize for the Most

Innovative Marketing Campaign for its imaginative steps in reaching out to the South Asian communities. A year later, the Society scooped the Excellence award at the Asian Jewel Awards. And, in 2004, the West Bromwich really scaled the pinnacle on diversity when it collected the Business in the Community's National Excellence Award from HRH Prince Charles at a prestigious occasion at the Royal Albert Hall.

The Society's Damian Johnson, Kiran Sharma and Jing Yee Harle join Chief Executive, Andrew Messenger, in banging the drum for Race for Opportunity.

The Society's Diversity Adviser, Bina Desai, collects the West Bromwich's National Excellence Award for Diversity from HRH Prince of Wales, Olympic gold medallist, Sir Steve Redgrave and Business in the Community's Julia Cleverdon.

As this roll call of success revealed, the West Bromwich had become a national pace-setter on diversity, a status that owed much to Andrew Messenger's passionate leadership and inspiring influence on diversity and racial equality. It was therefore only fitting that Andrew's outlook and decisive direction on diversity was rewarded. In 2001, Andrew was recognised by a special Editor's Award at the Mortgage Finance Gazette awards. In paying tribute to him, RfO's national director, Andrea Callender, expressed this glowing sentiment:

'It is impossible to over-estimate the contribution Andrew has made. If issues of equality and diversity are to be taken seriously, then we need champions with belief and energy to make this happen. Andrew, whose leadership has been inspirational, is an individual with those qualities in abundance.'

For Andrew, however, the award that gave him the greatest pleasure was when, in 2003 and in the succeeding year, the West Bromwich was named as one of the 100 Best Companies To Work For in the UK in the highly regarded *Sunday Times* survey. The biggest measure of job satisfaction in the country, the survey covered more than 47,000 employees in over 200 companies. Almost a third of the

The Society step up to receive their award after being named by the Sunday Times as one of the 100 Best Companies To Work For in the UK.

staff at the West Bromwich (250 people) voiced their opinions over a range of factors such as leadership, team spirit and a sense of well being. For Andrew, the unique appeal of this award was that it was staff themselves who were saying what a great place the West Bromwich Building Society was to work for and, above all, how they felt proud to be part of this confident, growing and forward-thinking business.

Chapter 8:

2006 and The Way Forward

The West Bromwich entered 2006 in formidable form with the Society again on course for another record year of financial results. Market conditions remained fiercely competitive and the Government's stringent regulation of the financial services industry in recent years had brought its own daunting challenges. Yet, as 2006 dawned, the West Bromwich had every reason to face the future with vigour and well-merited optimism. Nourished by the core values that had sustained the Society from the very day it was formed in 1849, guided by an unwavering vision, and equipped with an exciting and effective strategy, the horizon promised the bright prospect of continued growth and success.

Sadly, the beginning of the year was overshadowed by the death of Roger Dickens CBE, the Society's widely revered and popular chairman. Roger had been ill for some time, but his commitment to the Society never faltered and the tributes that poured in were testimony to the immense stature he occupied not only at the West Bromwich, but across the wider business community in the Midlands.

At a special memorial service for Roger at Birmingham's Symphony Hall in March 2006, Director General of the CBI, Sir Digby Jones, singled out Roger as 'a giant of a man' whose influence and impact would live on for the many individuals and organisations who had benefited from his wisdom, resilience and personal charm. Ian Brough, Chief Executive of the Black Country Chamber of Commerce, recollected Roger as 'a business icon, who championed so many important causes in the business world.' Mike Rake, senior partner of KPMG in the UK, where Roger first carved out his redoubtable reputation, referred to him as 'one of the outstanding partners of his generation.' For John James, head of the Institute of Directors in the West Midlands, Roger's death would leave 'an irreplaceable void in the West Midlands business world.'

Roger had been a past president of Birmingham Chamber of Commerce, chairman and founder of Birmingham Forward, UK deputy senior partner of accountancy giant KPMG, and instrumental in the phenomenal progress of iSoft where, during his tenure as Chairman, it grew to become the leading supplier of information systems to the health sector.

The respect Roger engendered extended well beyond the world of commerce and business. Awarded the CBE in 1991 Roger was later appointed to the position of Deputy Lieutenant for the West Midlands and, in 2005, received the prestigious title of High Sheriff of the County of West Midlands – a civic tribute

The Society's Chairman, Roger Dickens, was an outstanding figure,
held in the highest regard by all those who knew and worked with him.

of considerable standing and testament to the regard in which he was held at the highest levels.

This was the calibre of the man, who joined the Board of the West Bromwich in 1998, becoming Chairman the following year. In so many ways, Roger's attachment to the Society was rooted in the fact that he himself was born and raised in the Black Country. Indeed, he always retained a great affection for the region, proving a consistently powerful advocate on its behalf throughout his life.

During Roger's time at the West Bromwich the influence of his experience and expertise was clearly apparent. At Board level his incisive and cogent contributions were much in evidence during a period of exceptional progress for the Society. For staff who met him individually or heard him speaking at events such as Corporate Conferences or the Annual Dinner Dance, Roger will be remembered with affection for his good humour, kindness and consistent encouragement.

And for Chief Executive, Andrew Messenger, who came to know Roger well during the latter's time as Chairman of the Society, his poignant valediction captured Roger's many qualities: 'He was an absolute one-off. Apart from being a fountain of knowledge, he was a very special man and motivated all those around him. He made you feel 10ft tall as if there was nothing you couldn't do. Anyone who knew or worked with him knows they have been in the presence of a very special person.'

The loss of such an individual came as blow to all those who had worked with Roger but the West Bromwich was fortunate to have in Roger's successor a person of considerable distinction and status, someone possessing the attributes to help continue the Society's growing prowess.

Dr Brian Woods-Scawen was appointed as the new Chairman in February 2006. Brian had joined the Board as a non-executive director in January 2004 and his immediate and positive impression at the Society made him an ideal choice as Chairman in succession to Roger Dickens.

Brian Woods-Scawen takes up his position as the new Chairman of the West Bromwich.

That the West Bromwich had, in Brian Woods-Scawen, a man with impeccable leadership credentials was voiced by both Sir Digby Jones, Director General of the CBI, and the highly-respected figure of Sir Adrian Cadbury, formerly Chairman of Cadbury Schweppes and a previous Director of the Bank of England. In the words of Sir Digby Jones: 'I have known Brian as a business colleague and friend for many years. He is one of the leaders in the West Midlands business community. His strategic thinking is first-class and the Society could not have chosen anyone better.'

This glowing commendation was echoed by Sir Adrian Cadbury, himself a renowned authority on corporate governance. As Sir Adrian suggested: 'Brian is a superb professional, who is widely respected for his experience, knowledge and intellect. He has been at the forefront of several major initiatives across the West Midlands and has a great understanding of issues relating to the business community and the economic development of the region. For the West Bromwich, his clear-thinking and insight will add to the confidence and reputation of the Society as a progressive business.'

Sir Adrian's remarks cited Brian's work on corporate governance, which had been recognised at the highest level in 2004 when he was appointed by the Prime Minister to the Committee on Standards in Public Life. This national profile also saw Brian hold the position of an independent member on the Executive Board of the Department of Trade and Industry.

A Chartered Accountant by profession, Brian enjoyed a distinguished career at PricewaterhouseCoopers, where he was a member of the PwC Global Board and Chairman of the Midlands region. Brian's abilities and record of achievement meant he was much sought-after in many fields. He was widely applauded for his role in the economic and social regeneration of the West Midlands, including involvement in many of the region's largest and most complex deals, such as the acquisition of LDV by its management and employees and the expansion of Birmingham Airport.

Brian also had a staunch belief in education and skills improvement as a doorway to economic and personal development, as shown by his membership of the Council of Warwick University and his pioneering work in opening up opportunities in professional and financial services to ethnic minority communities.

Welcoming Brian to the post of Chairman, Andrew Messenger said: 'Brian is a high profile individual, greatly respected within the business community, who shares the ideals that we value so much at the West Bromwich. He will be a marvellous asset to the Society.'

On taking up his position, Brian issued this rallying call: 'I am committed to upholding our values because that is what holds us all together and creates our success. For over 150 years, the West Brom has served our members, our people and the communities in which we operate in a very special way and we will never allow that to change.'

Soon after, Brian was able to announce a further record-breaking performance for the West Bromwich as the financial year drew to a close in March

*Andrew Messenger, Chief Executive (standing), welcomes
the Society's new Chairman, Brian Woods-Scawen.*

2006. For the 9th consecutive year, the Society had excelled itself, surpassing even the previous year's lofty achievements.

The Society's assets now stood at £7.2 billion, which represented an astonishing growth of 23% on 2004-05. Mortgage assets were up a staggering 21% to a record £5.7 billion. Gross lending had risen 18% to a record £2.2 billion while net savings balances reached a record £4bn, an increase of £400 million. Subsidiaries also generated another impressive set of results, producing pre-tax profits of £18 million, up 21% from the previous high – almost half of the Group's profit of £38.5 million.

Above all, this magnificent Group performance translated into a record £30 million shared with members through better investment rates, loyalty mortgage rates and other mutuality benefits.

This is what mutuality should mean. Here, the West Bromwich was ahead of the field with its Privileged Membership Investment Account, which earned praise from leading commentator, Tony Hazel, Financial Editor of the Daily Mail for the unique way that it rewarded the loyalty of members according to their years of membership and number of products held. As he commented: 'Building societies have fought to prove mutuality can really deliver benefits. West Brom has tackled this problem head-on with its Privileged Membership Investment Account. This is a refreshing change from savings institutions. It's a progressive move and one from which other building societies should draw a lesson.' That

The Society's Deepa Parekh and James Taylor celebrate the Society's coveted Moneyfacts Award for Best Fixed-Rate Mortgage Provider (with redemption tie-in).

concept of mutuality was experienced also by borrowers through the Society's Privileged Membership mortgage discount, which is offered automatically to members who have had their mortgage with the Society for more than five years.

The Society's tremendous results were, indeed, a reason for celebration. Reporting on this remarkable portrait of success, one of the best in the whole of the building society sector, Chief Executive, Andrew Messenger, remarked: 'As a member business, we will never lose sight of the need to engage members and provide meaningful mutuality benefits to support the loyalty and trust they place in the West Brom. Everything we have done and plan to do is geared to protecting and promoting their best interests through a lifetime of good advice and value.'

As with all successful organisations, the West Bromwich was eager to guard against any notion of complacency. Already, as the new financial year began, the Society had constructed a comprehensive strategy with the overriding aim of giving members still greater value through higher savings rates, low mortgage rates, and professionally qualified one-to-one advice to help particularly with saving for retirement.

As the West Bromwich had repeatedly shown throughout its long and impressive history, having the imagination and capacity to adapt ensured the Society was well placed to respond to the varying and very individual needs of customers. That ability, for example, was seen in the growth of the intermediary side of the

The Society's Stephen Karle, Gary Cowdrill and David Barton
complete another major securitisation.

business and the increasing prominence of the Society's subsidiary companies. Profits generated by the non-member business can be used to reward members, primarily through lower mortgage and higher savings rates – a dynamic injection into the fluent and 'virtuous circle' of mutuality. Similarly with the Society's considered venture into the securitisation of commercial mortgage assets, which represented another reliable source of ongoing funding and a valuable device for supporting ambitious growth plans and balancing lending risk.

As Andrew Messenger concluded his report on yet another stunningly successful year by thanking members and staff for their wonderful loyalty and support, his sentiments were tinged by a real sense of sadness. This was to be the last time he would be composing his report in the role of Chief Executive of the West Bromwich. On 30th September 2006, Andrew will retire as Chief Executive and director of the Society.

In the history of the West Bromwich Building Society, Andrew Messenger emerges as a colossal figure in the Society's transformation from a business languishing in the doldrums, its very existence in peril, to an organisation that, on his departure, stood tall and self-confident as one of the country's top ten building societies. In outlining his contribution to the Society, Brian Woods-Scawen, Chairman of the West Bromwich, was unreserved in his praise: 'The success of the West Brom over the past decade is synonymous with the leadership, vitality and unceasing dedication of Andrew Messenger. Andrew has led from the front and has been fundamental in elevating the Society to one of the UK's major mutuals. He has been a superb ambassador for both the West Brom and the building society sector in general.'

During his ten years as Chief Executive, Andrew had presided over an unprecedented period of success for the West Bromwich. In that time, the Society's assets grew by nearly 500%; gross income up by 250%; profit increased by over 400%; gross lending rose by more than 500%; arrears dropped by nearly 85%; and mutuality benefits saw an astonishing 900% increase.

This has seen the Society return record results for nine consecutive years and deliver an industry-leading performance. Not only that, the Society's reputation has spread across the local and national stages with over 100 separate awards received since the turn of the Millennium, encompassing value-for-money products, customer service, staff welfare and satisfaction, diversity and community involvement.

Andrew himself was no stranger to the world of awards. Not only within the West Bromwich but externally, too, Andrew's star burned brightly. His expertise, knowledge and, most of all, inspirational leadership made him much in demand

The Society's Chief Executive, Andrew Messenger, announces another
year of outstanding results for the West Bromwich.

from numerous bodies. A Fellow of the Chartered Institute of Bankers, Member of Business in the Community's Regional Leadership Team, formerly Regional Council Member of the CBI, Chair of Race for Opportunity in the West Midlands, National Council Member of the Building Societies Association, and Director of the Black Country Consortium – wherever he was asked to serve, Andrew unfailingly gave of his best and evoked the highest praise.

In 2001, Andrew received the Mortgage Finance Gazette Editor's Award; in 2002 Mortgage Finance Gazette gave Andrew the prestigious Leadership Award; in 2005 Andrew collected the Black Country Chamber Business Leaders Award and President's Special Award for Enterprise. The hallmarks of leadership – an astute business acumen allied to a fervent belief that people really matter – which Andrew displayed with such distinction led the University of Central England to award him an Honorary Doctorate in 2005. In particular, Andrew was lauded for his exemplary record in business and for his dedication to diversity and racial equality. Later that year, the University of Wolverhampton also awarded Andrew an Honorary Doctorate of Business Administration. This time the citation heralded Andrew's innovative approach to staff motivation and customer service.

Andrew receives the title of Lord of the Manor of West Bromwich
from football legend, Sir Bobby Charlton.

Andrew had certainly come a long way from that council house in Sandbach, Cheshire – a lifetime's journey of achievement and accolades. But perhaps the most visible illumination of how far Andrew had come took place in February 2005 when he was named Lord of the Manor of West Bromwich, a notional title bestowed on individuals who have had a significant impact on the town. In so many ways, this title epitomised the way West Bromwich regarded Andrew Messenger as an adopted son of the town. And how special, too, for Andrew that he was given the award by his boyhood hero, Sir Bobby Charlton, in a glittering ceremony attended by family, friends and dignitaries from the worlds of business, education, sport and entertainment.

Andrew is certainly a hard act to follow, but if the watchword is continuity then the West Bromwich has in new Chief Executive, Stephen Karle, who takes up the position on 1st October 2006, an individual with the pedigree and all-round qualities to maintain that momentum of success. Importantly, Stephen is a man versed in the values and style of the West Bromwich, having joined in 1995 as Secretary to the Society. Previously Stephen had worked as a solicitor at a major law firm where he was widely admired as an influential figure within the regional business community.

Stephen was appointed to the Board of the Society in 2000 with additional responsibility for business risk, compliance, efficiency and IT. His accomplished performance in delivering on objectives led to his further promotion in 2004 when Stephen was made Operations Director. As a result, he assumed an extensive portfolio of responsibilities, notably sales, marketing and distribution, business operations and people recruitment and development.

With a renowned vision and versatility, Stephen's flair and enthusiasm have been key elements in the capacity of the Society to respond effectively and swiftly to an intensely competitive and rapidly changing market, especially one where the operating environment is characterised by increasing regulation. What also marks out Stephen as an individual well-suited to the challenge of Chief Executive is his willingness to innovate, together with his ability to motivate staff and harness the potential of everyone at the West Bromwich. Like his predecessor, Stephen shares that same admiration for the Society's tremendous team spirit, skill and irrepressible enthusiasm and the care people show towards customers and each other.

With Stephen Karle at the helm the Society can rest assured it has an individual with the determination and outlook to work tirelessly in leading the Society into an era of sustained success.

In its Summary Corporate Plan 2006–2009 the West Bromwich Building Society has the avowed mission to become the best performing building society with 'leading mutuality benefits provided through a trusted brand for advice, value and service.' A bold assertion, but if we see the distance the Society has travelled since those humble days back in 1849 when the founding fathers of the West Bromwich took their first steps towards securing a better and dignified tomorrow for ordinary people, then the vision of Growing – Thriving – Sharing will guide the Society on towards attaining that noble goal.

Above: Stephen Karle (right) is congratulated on his appointment as the Society's new Chief Executive by Andrew Messenger, the retiring Chief Executive, and (centre) Brian Woods-Scawen, Chairman of the Society.

Left: The West Bromwich's new Chief Executive, Stephen Karle.

Appendix

A selection of the many charitable and community organisations helped by the West Bromwich Building Society over the past decade:

Acorns Children's Trust
Action & Research for Multiple Sclerosis
Action Heart, Russell's Hall Hospital
African Caribbean Cultural Initiative, Wolverhampton
Air Training Corps
Alexandra High School Young Enterprise Initiative
Beacon Centre for the Blind
Birmingham Children's Hospice
Birmingham Children's Hospital
Birmingham Royal Institute for the Blind
Birmingham Transport Museum
Birmingham Trust for Psychotherapy
Birmingham Youth Dance Company
Brant Pianoforte Competition
Breast Cancer Care
British Heart Foundation
British Red Cross
Cancer Research UK
Cancer Research at Birmingham
Cannock Scouts
Children in Need
Children with Leukaemia
Comic Relief Red Nose Day
Compton Hospice
Cradley Heath Male Voice Choir
County Air Ambulance
Dartmouth High School
Dial-a-Ride Santa Run
Diocese of Lichfield's Church Urban Fund
Dudley Cave Rescue Team
Duke of Edinburgh Award Scheme
Fairbridge Project
Guide Dogs for the Blind Association
Handsworth Schools Cricket Tournament
Healthy Sandwell Bike Ride

Help the Aged
Helping Hands
Hillcrest School and Community College
Holly Hall School, Dudley
Hope House Hospice, Newtown
Imperial Cancer Research
Kidney Research UK
Kids Out Charity
Llandysilio Church School, Powys
Lord Taverner's Cricket Coaching Scheme
MacMillan Nurses Appeal
Manchester Cathedral Bomb Damage Repair Fund
Marie Curie Cancer Care
Mary Stephen's Hospice, Stourbridge
Menzies High School
Montgomeryshire Wildlife Trust
Myton Park Hospice, Leamington
NCH Action for Children
New Cross Hospital Children's Ward
Newport Sports Centre Appeal
NSPCC
Old Park Special School, Dudley
Oswestry Radio Link Community Safety
Outward Bound Trust
Pendeford Mill Nature Reserve
People's Dispensary for Sick Animals
Perton Playgroup
Royal Orthopaedic Hospital
Sandwell Aid
Sandwell Alzheimer's Society
Sandwell Neighbourhood Watch
Sandwell NHS Healthcare Trust
Sandwell Women's Aid
Sandwell Women's Agency Network
Sandwell Young Carers
Sense
Shelter
Shropshire and Mid-Wales Hospice
Sir Steve Redgrave Trust
South Bromsgrove Community High School
St Bartholomew's Church, Wednesbury
St Mary the Virgin Restoration Fund, Hillcrest
St Mary's Hospice, Birmingham
St Paul's Church, Birmingham

Stonehouse Gang Youth Scheme
Superschool Quiz
Sutton Community Sailing Club
Swan Village and Carter's Green Goldies
Swan Village Action Group
Torch Appeal, Oswestry
Ty Hafren Children's Hospice, Cardiff
VICTA
Tsunami Emergency Disaster Appeal
Variety Club of Great Britain
Warley Male Voice Choir Charity Concerts
Warley Woods Community Trust
Water Aid
Welshpool Victoria Hospital
West Bromwich Albion Community Programme
West Midlands Crime Stoppers
Whizz Kids
Wolverhampton Rotary Club
Wolverhampton Town Show
World Expedition Challenge
Y-Care International

Assets	£
1859	22,107
1869	70,098
1879	170,223
1889	165,470
1899	154,719
1909	208,802
1919	294,463
1929	789,087
1939	3,767,299
1949	5,102,712
1959	13,028,684
1969	37,546,433
1979	216,275,132
1989	715,225,000
1999	2,408,000,000
2006	7,207,800,000

Awards

The West Bromwich has won numerous awards in recent years. Here are just some of the major awards the Society has received since 2000:

2006	Moneyfacts Awards	Top Fixed Rate Mortgage Provider
2006	Race for Opportunity	Runner-up in national survey
2005	Mortgage Strategy Technology Service Awards	Gold Standard
2005	UK Business Excellence Awards	Special Award for Business Employee Satisfaction
2005	Moneyfacts Awards	Best Self-Certification Mortgage Provider
2005	Race for Opportunity	Gold Standard
2005	Mortgage Strategy Awards	Mortgage Force – Best Broker
2005	Variety Club Awards	Best Business Working in the Community
2005	Personnel Today Awards	Best Overall Company
2004	Financial Adviser Awards	Mortgage Lenders
2004	Mitial Call Centre Awards	Best Contact Centre in West Midlands
2004	BiTC Awards for Excellence	Diversity Award
2003	Best of Black Country Awards	Business of the Year
2003	Personnel Today	Managing Health at Work
2003	Black Country Chamber Business Awards	Special Award for Enterprise
2003	Asian Jewel Awards	Excellence in Diversity
2003	Institute of Financial Services	Most Innovative Marketing Campaign
2002	Windrush Achievement Award	Gold Standard
2002	Midlands Business Excellence Awards	Large Company Award
2002	Midlands Business Excellence Awards	Equal Opportunities Employer Award
2001	Kids Out Community Award	Community Winner
2001	Human Resources Magazine	Excellence in the Community
2001	Rotary Club of Great Britain	Community Award
2000	Sandwell and Dudley MBC	Company of the Year
2000	Midlands Business Excellence Awards	Best Large Company
2000	Midlands Business Excellence Awards	Best Business in the Community
2000	Mortgage Finance Gazette	Community Award
2000	Birmingham Chamber of Commerce	Outstanding Customer Service
2000	3b (Black Business in Birmingham)	Corporate Responsibility Award

From Little Acorns Grow

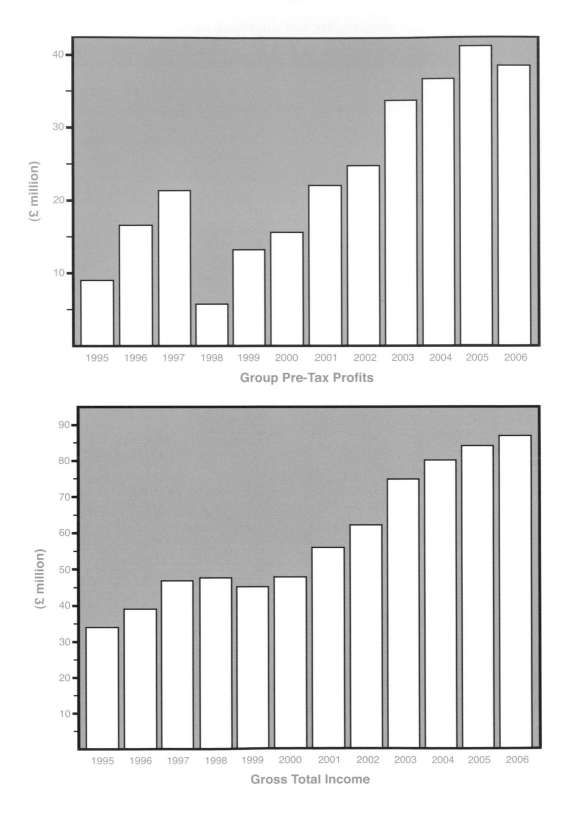

(£ million)

40

30

20

10

| 1995 | 1996 | 1997 | 1998 | 1999 | 2000 | 2001 | 2002 | 2003 | 2004 | 2005 | 2006 |

Group Pre-Tax Profits

(£ million)

90

80

70

60

50

40

30

20

10

| 1995 | 1996 | 1997 | 1998 | 1999 | 2000 | 2001 | 2002 | 2003 | 2004 | 2005 | 2006 |

Gross Total Income

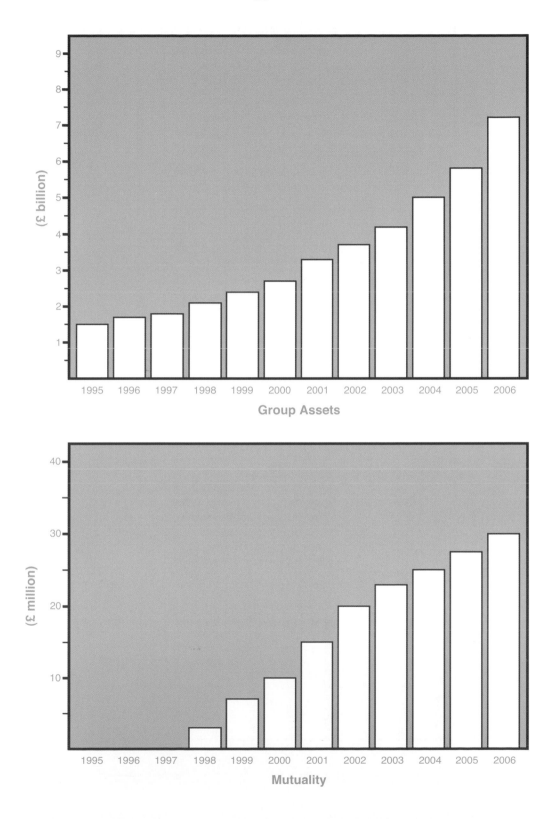

Group Assets

Mutuality

Chief Executive Officers

1849 - 1859	Secretary: James Sharp
1859 - 1902	Secretary: John Hampton
1902 - 1903	Secretary: Thomas Hampton
1903 - 1905	Secretary: James Coleman
1905 - 1936	Secretary: John Garbett
1936 - 1961	Managing Director & Secretary: John Scott Wright
1961 - 1983	Managing Director: Frank Dilkes
1983 - 1985	Managing Director: Leslie Tinkler
1985 - 1988	General Manager & Secretary: Michael Price
1988 - 1991	Managing Director: Jeffrey Allard
1991 - 1996	Chief Executive: Glenn Elliot
1996 - 2006	Chief Executive: Andrew Messenger
2006 -	Chief Executive: Stephen Karle

The Society's Presidents and Chairmen

1849 - 1898	President: Reuben Farley (First Mayor of West Bromwich)
1898 - 1916	President: John Horton Blades (First MP for West Bromich)
1916 - 1922	President: John Marston
1922 - 1927	President: Edward Arnold (Mayor of West Bromwich)
1927 - 1946	President: Thomas Cottrell (Mayor of West Bromwich)
1946 - 1963	President: Frederick Stamps
1963 - 1983	President: Bernard Smith (Title changed to Chairman 1970)
1983 - 1990	Chairman: Frank Dilkes
1990 - 1992	Chairman: Thomas Turner
1992 - 1998	Chairman: John Baker
1998 - 1999	Chairman: Raymond Dickinson
1999 - 2006	Chairman: Roger Dickens CBE
2006 -	Chairman: Dr Brian Woods-Scawen
1985 - 1987	Honorary President: Bernard Smith
1987 - 1992	Honorary President: Cecil Ellmore

End Notes

End Notes: Chapter 1

[1] John Alfred Langford (ed), *A Century of Birmingham Life or A Chronicle of Local Events from 1741 to 1841* (Birmingham: 1868), p. 201.

[2] S. J. Price, *Building Societies. Their Origin and History* (London: 1952), p. 102.

[3] William Hutton, *History of Birmingham* (Birmingham: 1795), p. 211.

[4] Price, *Building Societies*, p. 27.

[5] Price, *Building Societies*, p. 30 and *Aris's Birmingham Gazette*, 18 February 1782, cited in E.J. Cleary, *The Building Society Movement* (London: 1965), p. 13.

[6] M.W. Beresford, 'The Back-to-Back House in Leeds, 1787-1937', in, Stanley D. Chapman (ed), *The History of Working-class Housing: A Symposium* (Newton Abbot: 1971), p. 102.

[7] S.D. Chapman and J.N. Bartlett, 'The Contribution of Building Clubs and Freehold Land Society to Working-Class Housing in Birmingham, in, Chapman (ed), *The History of Working-class Housing*, pp. 236-7.

[8] Cleary, *The Building Society Movement*, pp. 13 and 22.

[9] Harold Bellman, *The Building Society Movement* (London: 1927), p. 10.

[10] Cleary, *The Building Society Movement*, pp. 47-9.

[11] G.J. Johnson, 'Statistics of the Benefit, and Building, and Freehold Land Societies in Birmingham' (1865), in, John Edward Langford (ed), *Modern Birmingham and its Institutions. A Chronicle of Local Events from 1841 to 1871, Volume II* (Birmingham: 1871), p. 165.

[12] Cleary, *The Building Society Movement*, p. 49.

[13] Chapman and Bartlett, 'The Contribution of Building Clubs', p. 239.

[14] John Edward Langford (ed), *Modern Birmingham and its Institutions. A Chronicle of Local Events from 1841 to 1871, Volume II*, (Birmingham: 1871), p. 161.

[15] *The Prospectus of the Birmingham Freehold Land Society* (seventh edition).

[16] F.W. Hackwood, *History of West Bromwich*.

[17] D. Dilworth, *West Bromwich Before the Industrial Revolution* (Halesowen: 1973).

[18] Arthur Young, *Tours in England and Wales*, cited in W.H.B. Court, *The Rise of the Midland Industries, 1600-1838* (London: 1938), p. 195.

[19] W.E. Jephcott, *House of Izons* (1948), p. 46.

[20] R.A. Church, Kenricks in Hardware. *A Family Business, 1791-1966* (Newton Abbott: 1969), p. 28.

[21] Dave Reeves (compiled and ed), *Cardboard Crowns & Cast Iron Cookpots* (West Bromwich: 1996), p. 48.

[22] J. Pigot, *New Commercial Directory of Staffordshire* (1829), p. 752.

[23] Harry Bayliss, *Christ Church West Bromwich 1829-1929* (West Bromwich: 1928), p. 10.

[24] William Kenrick, 'Cast Iron Hollow-Ware, Tinned and Enamelled, and Cast Ironmongery', in, Samuel Timmins (ed), *Birmingham and the Midland Hardware District* (London: 1866), p. 108.

[25] Colin Giles, *Birmingham and Wolverhampton Box Iron Makers* (unpublished ms: no date).

26   The Chemistry of Progress. Robinson Brothers Limited (London: 1969).

27   Elihu Burrit, *Walks in the Black Country* (1st published 1868, London: 1976 edn) p. 182

28   H.H. Prince, *The Romance of Early Methodism in and around West Bromwich and Wednesbury* (West Bromwich: 1925), pp. 55-9.

29   J.F.C. Harrison, 'Methodism', in, John Cannon (ed), *The Oxford Companion to British History* (Oxford: 1997), p. 639.

30   For the information on occupations of the founding members of the West Bromwich Permanent Society I am indebted to the following librarians at Smethwick Library who scoured trades directories and census returns for me: Maureen Waldron, Sam Goode, Claire Harrington, Dawn Winter and especially Helen Knight.

31   Henry Herbert Prince, *Old West Bromwich or the Story of Long Ago* (West Bromwich: 1924), pp. 121-3.

32   H.H. Prince, *The Romance of Early Methodism*, pp. 47-8.

33   Prince, *Old West Bromwich*, p. 123.

34   *Second Annual Report of the West Bromwich Building Society* (31 May 1851).

35   *Seventh Annual Report* (14 April 1856).

36   *Third Annual Report* (19 April 1852).

37   *Fourth Annual Report* (18 April 1853).

38   *Thirteenth Annual Report* (9 May 1862).

39   *Ninth Annual Report* (13 May 1857).

40   *Building Societies Who's Who* (London: 1955/56), p. 350.

41   *Eighth Annual Report* (13 April 1857).

42   Kenrick, 'Cast Iron Hollow-Ware', p. 109.

43   E.I. Davies, 'Hand-made Nail Trade of Birmingham and District' (The University of Birmingham M.Com. thesis, 1933), p. 191.

44   David Christie Murray, 'A Capful O' Nails' (1st published 1879, Halesowen: 1973 edn); for a discussion of Murray see R.D. Woodall, *West Bromwich Yesterdays. A Short Historical Study of 'The City of a Hundred Trades'* (Sutton Coldfield: 1958), pp. 76-83.

45   *Second Annual Report* (31 May 1851).

46   *Building Societies Who's Who*, p. 347.

47   *Thirty-Sixth Annual Report* (22 June 1885).

47   *Third Annual Report* (19 April 1852).

49   *Fifth Annual Report* (22 May 1854); and *Sixth Annual Report* (16 April 1855).

50   *Sixth Annual Report* (16 April 1855); and *Ninth Annual Report* (12 April 1858).

End Notes: Chapter 2

1   *Eleventh Annual Report* (14 May 1860); and *Thirteenth Annual Report* (9 May 1862).

2   *Eleventh Annual Report* (14 May 1860);

3   *Twelfth Annual Report* (11 May 1861).

4   *Twenty-Sixth Annual Report* (5 June 1875).

5   *Twenty-Ninth Annual Report* (15 June 1878); and *Twenty-Third Annual Report* (8 June 1872).

6   *Building Society Who's Who*, p. 345; and *Twenty-Seventh Annual Report* (17 June 1876).

7   *Thirtieth Annual Report* (11 June 1879).

8   *Thirty-Second Annual Report* (25 June 1881).

9   *Thirty-Third Annual Report* (26 June 1882); *Thirty-Fourth Annual Report* (23 June 1883); and *Thirty-Fifth Annual Report* (23 June 1884).

10   Martin Boddy, *The Building Societies* (London: 1980), p. 10.

[11] *Fortieth Annual Report* (17 June 1889); and *Fifty-Sixth Annual Report* (9 June 1905).

[12] *Thirty-Fifth Annual Report* (23 June 1884); and *Twenty-First Annual Report* (13 June 1870).

[13] *Thirty-Seventh Annual Report* (21 June 1886).

[14] *Thirty-Ninth Annual Report* (18 June 1888).

[15] *Forty-First Annual Report* (16 June 1890).

[16] *Forty-Third Annual Report* (13 June 1892).

[17] *Forty-Fourth Annual Report* (12 June 1893); and *Forty-Fifth Annual Report* (11 June 1894).

[18] Bellman, *The Building Society Movement*, p. 14.

[19] Cleary, *The Building Society Movement*, pp. 141-5.

[20] Bellman, *The Building Society Movement*, p.19.

[21] *Forty-Fourth Annual Report* (12 June 1893).

[22] *Forty-Seventh Annual Report* (3 June 1896).

[23] Cleary, *The Building Society Movement*, pp. 101-115.

[24] *Forty-Eighth Annual Report* (1 June 1897).

[25] *Forty-Ninth Annual Report* (25 May 1898).

[26] *Fiftieth Annual Report* (14 June 1899).

[27] *Fifty-First Annual Report* (7 June 1900).

[28] *Fifty-Second Annual Report* (13 June 1901).

[29] *Fifty-Sixth Annual Report* (9 June 1905); and *Forty-Seventh Annual Report* (3 June 1896).

[30] 'Charges of Robbery and Embezzlement against the Secretary of the Smethwick Building Society', *The Free Press*, 24 March 1883

[31] See Cleary, *The Building Society Movement*, pp. 122-7.

[32] *Fifty-Sixth Annual Report* (9 June 1905).

[33] *Fifty-Seventh Annual Report* (6 June 1906); and *Fifty-Eighth Annual Report* (7 June 1907).

[34] *Fifty-Ninth Annual Report* (4 June 1908).

[35] *Sixty-First Annual Report* (3 June 1910).

[36] Glyn Davies, *Building Societies and their Branches – a Regional Economic Survey* (London: 1981) p. 32.

[37] *Sixty-Fourth Annual Report* (11 June 1914).

[38] *Second Annual Report* (31 May 1851).

[39] *Fifteenth Annual Report* (20 May 1864).

[40] Cleary, *The Building Society Movement*, p. 68.

[41] *Seventeenth Annual Report* (21 May 1866).

[42] *Eighteenth Annual Report* (3 June 1867).

[43] *Twentieth Annual Report* (31 May 1869).

[44] *Twenty-First Annual Report* (13 June 1870).

[45] *Thirtieth Annual Report* (11 June 1879).

[46] *Thirty-Second Annual Report* (25 June 1881).

[47] *Forty-Second Annual Report* (12 June 1891).

[48] *Forty-Third Annual Report* (13 June 1892).

[49] *Second Annual Report* (31 May 1851).

[50] *Fifty-Third Annual Report* (13 June 1902).

[51] *Fifty-Fourth Annual Report* (11 June 1903).

[52] *West Bromwich Permanent Benefit Building Society, Prospectus* (1909).

[53] *Eighth Annual Report* (13 May 1857).

[54] *Thirty-Fourth Annual Report* (23 June 1883); and *Forty-First Annual Report* (16 June 1890).

[55] *Thirty-Eighth Annual Report* (20 June 1887); and *Forty-Ninth Annual Report* (25 May 1898).

[56] *West Bromwich Permanent Benefit Building Society, Prospectus* (1909).

[57] *Fifty-Third Annual Report* (13 June 1902)

[58] *West Bromwich Permanent Benefit Building Society* (1898), thanks to Mr. K. Jukes.

[59] *Sixth Annual Report* (16 April 1855).

[60] *Fifteenth Annual Report* (20 May 1864).

[61] *Twenty-Third Annual Report* (8 June 1872).

[62] *Twenty-Fourth Annual Report* (6 June 1873).

[63] *Fifty-Third Annual Report* (13 June 1902).

[64] *Fifty-Fourth Annual Report* (11 June 1903).

[65] *Eleventh Annual Report* (14 May 1860).

[66] *Thirty-Third Annual Report* (26 June 1882).

[67] *Twenty-Fourth Annual Report* (6 June 1873).

[68] *Rules of the West Bromwich Permanent Benefit Building Society* (West Bromwich: 1914), p. 23.

[69] Margaret Lincoln, *A Sketch of the Life of Samuel Withers* (unpublished ms: 28 April 1982). A full account of the Withers family is in Geoffrey William Withers and Margaret Beryl Lincoln, *The Withers of West Bromwich. An Exercise in Genealogy and Local History* (unpublished ms: 1981). I am grateful to Margaret Lincoln for sight of this material.

[70] *Nineteenth Annual Report* (1 June 1868).

[71] *Rules*, pp. 23-4.

[72] Cited in Cleary, *The Building Society Movement*, p. 91.

[73] *Twelfth Annual Report* (9 May 1861).

[74] *Fourteenth Annual Report* (22 May 1863).

[75] *Seventeenth Annual Report* (21 May 1866).

[76] *Thirty-Sixth Annual Report* (22 June 1885).

[77] *Twenty-Fifth Annual Report* (5 June 1874).

[78] *Thirty-Second Annual Report* (25 June 1881).

[79] 'Alderman Reuben Farley J.P.', *Midland Chronicle* (20 November 1896). I am grateful to Thelma Prentice, librarian at Thimblemill Library, for providing me with this and other articles concerning Reuben Farley and also John Horton Blades.

[80] 'Mr Reuben Farley J.P., First Mayor of West Bromwich', *Free Press* (24 March 1883).

[81] 'Alderman Reuben Farley J.P.', *Midland Chronicle* (20 November 1896).

[82] *The Free Press*, 24 April 1896.

[83] 'The Passing of Farley', *The Chronicle* 17 March 1899.

[84] 'Mr Reuben Farley J.P., First Mayor of West Bromwich', *Free Press* (24 March 1883).

[85] 'The Passing of Farley', *The Chronicle* 17 March 1899.

[86] *Forty-Ninth Annual Report* (24 May 1898).

[87] *Fiftieth Annual Report* (14 June 1899).

[88] 'Alderman Blades J.P.', *Midland Chronicle* (8 January 1897).

[89] 'Alderman Blades J.P.', *Midland Chronicle* (8 January 1897)

[90] *Fiftieth Annual Report* (14 June 1899); and *Fifty-Second Annual Report* (13 June 1901).

[91] *Sixty-Sixth Annual Report* (10 June 1915).

[92] 'Death of Alderman Blades', *Midland Chronicle* (14 April 1916).

End Notes: Chapter 3

1 Cleary, *The Building Society Movement*, pp. 170-12.
2 *Sixty-Sixth Annual Report* (10 June 1915).
3 *Sixty-Seventh Annual Report* (25 May 1916).
4 *Sixty-Eighth Annual Report* (31 May 1917).
5 Davies, *Building Societies and Their Branches*, p. 41.
6 *Forty-Third Annual Report* (13 June 1892); *Sixty-Fifth Annual Report* (11 June 1914); and *Sixty-Ninth Annual Report* (6 June 1918).
7 Newspaper cutting, 1921.
8 'West Bromwich Building Society', *Midland Chronicle*, 10 June 1918.
9 'West Bromwich Building Society', *The Free Press*, 10 June 1918.
10 British Association for the Advancement of Science, *Birmingham and its Regional Setting: A Scientific Survey* (Birmingham: 1950), p. 254.
11 Woodall, *West Bromwich Yesterdays*, p. 36.
12 Carl Chinn, *Homes For People: 100 Years of Council Housing in Birmingham* (Birmingham Books: 1991), pp. 43-4.
13 'All-Round Increases', newspaper cutting, 1935.
14 'Jacob Faithful', newspaper cutting, 1927.
15 I thank Paul Turner for this information taken from the *Handbook of the National Association of Building Societies* (London: 1927).
16 'All-Round Increases', newspaper cutting, 1935.
17 Leslie Pearce, 'letter', 19 August 1998. Thanks to Tim Dyson for this information.
18 Emily and James Pardoe, 'Letter', 1998.
19 'West Bromwich Permanent Building Society's New Head Offices', *Birmingham Gazette*, 7 January 1928.
20 'West Bromwich Building Society', newspaper cutting, 15 June 1929.
21 West Bromwich Building Society. 'List of Districts in which Mortgaged Properties are Situated' (January 1930). I thank Philip May for this reference.
22 Olive V. Patrick, 'Letter', 25 June 1998.
23 'West Bromwich Building Society', *Free Press* (10 June 1918).
24 'Borrowers Wanted', *Midland Chronicle*, 29 May 1936.
25 'The West Bromwich Stone-Laying Ceremony', *Midland Chronicle*, 12 November 1926.
26 'Mainstay of the Working Classes', *Midland Chronicle and Free Press*, 26 February 1937.
27 'Building Societies Protecting Welfare of Working People', *The Weekly News*, 27 February 1937.
28 'Assets of Nearly £3,000,000', *Birmingham Post*, 16 May 1938.
29 'West Bromwich Permanent Benefit Building Society's New Head Offices', *Birmingham Gazette*, 7 January 1928; and 'Mr John Garbett', *Midland Chronicle and Free Press*, 20 March 1936.
30 'Municipalities and Building Societies', newspaper cutting, 1932.
31 'Royal Recognition for Building Societies', *Smethwick Telephone*, 27 May 1933.
32 'Another 5 Per Cent. for Shareholders', newspaper cutting, 1925.
33 'West Bromwich Building Society', *Free Press*, 12 November 1926.
34 West Bromwich Building Society, *Prospectus* (1931).
35 'Formal Opening of New Offices', *Birmingham Post*, 2 January 1928.
36 'West Bromwich Permanent Building Society's New Head Offices', *Birmingham Gazette*, 7 January 1928.

37 'How Homes are Provided for the People', *Smethwick Telephone*, 6 January 1928.
38 'A Flourishing Society', newspaper cutting, 1928.
39 Newspaper cutting, 1928.
40 Frank Dilkes, managing director, 'Letter to Miss J.F.G. Albanesius', 19 March 1982.
41 'Death of Mr John Marston', *West Bromwich Free Press*, 8 February 1929. I am grateful to Thelma Prentice of Thimblemill Library for this reference.
42 'Funeral of Alderman Arnold', *The Free Press*, 17 June 1922; see also Mike Kelly, 'Notes on a conversation with Mrs. Davies', 5 May 1998. Mrs. Davies is the daughter of Edward Arnold.
43 *West Bromwich Permanent Benefit Building Society. Enrolled according to Act of Parliament*, 25 May 1928.
44 *Eightieth Annual General Meeting* (11 June 1929).
45 'Royal Recognition for Building Societies', *Smethwick Telephone*, 27 May 1933.
46 'Presentation to West Bromwich Auditor', *Midland Chronicle*, 9 May 1936.
47 'Here and There', *Smethwick Telephone*, 29 May 1933; Woodall, *West Bromwich*, p. 29.
48 *Eighty-Fifth Annual General Meeting* (18 May 1934).
49 *Eighty-Seventh Annual General Meeting* (15 May 1936)
50 'Mr John Garbett', *Midland Chronicle and Free Press*, 20 March 1936; for training of staff see 'West Bromwich Building Society', 15 June 1929, newspaper cutting; and for superannuation fund see 'West Bromwich Building Society', *Free Press*, 30 May 1930 and 'West Bromwich Building Society', *Smethwick Telephone* (19 May 1934).
51 'A Flourishing Society', newspaper cutting, 1928.
52 *Twenty-Third Annual Report* (10 June 1871).
53 'A Flourishing Society', newspaper cutting, 1928.
54 *Prospectus*, p.2.
55 *Rules of the West Bromwich Building Society* (c. 1931), p. 10.
56 *Prospectus*, pp. 4-9.
57 'West Bromwich Building Society', newspaper cutting, 1931; 'West Bromwich Building Society', newspaper cutting, 15 June 1929; and *Eighty-Third Annual General Meeting* (13 May 1932).
58 'West Bromwich Building Society', newspaper cutting, 1932.
59 *Eighty-Fourth Annual General Meeting* (12 May 1933), p. 2.
60 Phyllis W. Adams, 'Letter', 24 June 1998.
61 Joan M. McDonald, 'Letter', 25 May 1998; and *Seventy-First Annual Report*, 4 June 1920.
62 *Rules* (1914), p. 10.
63 'A Three Million Society', *Smethwick Telephone*, 28 May 1938.
64 'Building Society Receipts Past £2,000,000 Mark', *Birmingham Gazette*, 24 May 1939.

End Notes: Chapter 4

1 Mark Boléat, *The Building Society Industry* (London: 1982), p. 4.
2 Cited in Boddy, *The Building Societies*, p. 14.
3 'West Bromwich Building Society', newspaper cutting, June 1929.
4 Davies, *Building Societies*, p. 50.
5 *The Centenary of the West Bromwich Building Society, 1849-1949* (West Bromwich: 1949), p. 8; and 'West Bromwich Building Society', *Midland Chronicle*, 15 May 1942.
6 'Building Society Does Not Begrudge Income Tax', *Weekly News*, 22 May 1942.
7 'Mr John Garbett's Death', newspaper cutting, 1946; and Woodall, *West Bromwich Yesterdays*, p. 42.

8 Information on Ruby Greathead supplied by Nigel Newman, 10 October 1998.

9 Joan M. McDonald, 'Letter', 25 May 1998.

10 'West Bromwich Building Society', *Midland Chronicle*, 26 June 1944.

11 'Building Society Tax Rate Going Up', *Sunday Despatch*, 11 May 1947.

12 *The Centenary*, p. 12.

13 'Assets Top Six Million Pounds', *Midland Chronicle*, 2 June 1950.

14 'Gossip of the Week', *Midland Chronicle*, 8 March 1946; and 'Obituary', *Midland Chronicle*, 19 July 1963. I am grateful to Thelma Prentice of Thimblemill Library for this reference.

15 'Assets Top Six Million Pounds', *Midland Chronicle*, 2 June 1950.

16 Boddy, *The Building Societies*, p. 17.

17 Cleary, *The Building Society Movement*, p. 249.

18 *Building Societies' Who's Who*, pp. 372-5, 370, 351, 355-6, 368, 369, 359 and 354.

19 West Bromwich Building Society, 'Armorial Bearings'.

20 'Obituary', *Midland Chronicle*, 19 July 1963.

21 Boddy, *The Building Societies*, pp. 18-21.

22 Stephen Karle, 'Notes on a Meeting with Mr. Les Tinkler', 1 October 1998.

23 Frank P. Dilkes, 'Letter to Carl Chinn', 4 August 1998.

24 S. Karle, 'Notes on a Meeting with Mr. Les Tinkler', 1 October 1998.

25 West Bromwich Building Society, *Directors' Reports* (8 May 1968).

26 'West Bromwich Building Society Opens New Branch in Welshpool', *County Times and Express Gazette*, 8 May 1971.

27 *One-Hundred-and Twenty-Ninth Annual Report* (31 March 1978).

28 Davies, *Building Societies*, pp. 86-7.

29 S. Karle, 'Notes on a Meeting with Mr. Les Tinkler', 1 October 1998.

30 Frank Dilkes, managing director, 'Letter to Miss J.F.G. Albanesius', 19 March 1982.

31 'A £20m. Building Society', newspaper cutting, c. 1962.

32 Honorary Alderman Mrs. Freda Cocks O.B.E., J.P., 'Letter to Carl Chinn', 21 April 1997.

33 Sue Bartleet-Cross, 'Diary of an Ex-Branch Employee' (August 1998).

34 Davies, *Building Societies*, p. 108.

35 'West Bromwich Building Society', *Sunday Mercury*, 12 November 1978.

36 'West Bromwich Building Society', *Evening Mail*, 3 November 1978.

37 Nigel Newman, 'Interview with John Kent', 19 October 1998.

38 'The Fed Up, Happy Workers . . .', *Sandwell Evening Mail*, 22 March 1979.

39 'Letters via Bradford', *Sunday Mercury*, 8 July 1979.

40 'Triple Foundation', *Birmingham Post*, 14 September 1978.

End Notes: Chapter 5

1 Davies, *Building Societies*, pp. 180-182

2 'Home Loans for Special Cases Only', Evening Mail, 7 January 1974; and 'Building Society Considers Bonus', *Birmingham Post*, 1 April 1976.

3 Boléat, *The Building Society Industry*, pp. 33 and 21.

4 'Goodbye to the Chair at 91', *Evening Mail*, 11 August 1983.

5 'Society Grows as Enterprise Continues', *Evening Mail*, 3 August 1983.

6 'Societies Move into Banking', *Birmingham Post*, 4 April 1978.

7 'Building Society Starts Pensions', *Evening Mail*, 16 April 1982.

8 'Firms Form Team to Widen Markets', *Birmingham Post*, 30 September 1986; *Birmingham Post*, 15 May 1988.

[9] Building Society Cuts Agency Link', *Birmingham Post,* 4 May 1989; 'Managers Move Up', *Birmingham Post,* 6 June 1989; and *Birmingham Post,* 30 August 1989.

[10] 'Steel Strikers Mortgage Plea', *Evening Mail,* 3 March 1980.

[11] Ray Smith, '£2m for Tenants Who Want to Buy', *Evening Mail,* 10 January 1984; and 'Aid for Council Tenants', *Evening Mail,* 5 February 1983.

[12] West Bromwich Building Society, *Network News,* August 1982.

[13] Network News, January 1983.

[14] 'Advertising Feature', *Sandwell Evening Mail,* 14 August 1981.

[15] '"New-Look" Branch Open', *Evening Mail,* 3 August 1983.

[16] 'Have-a-go Hero Chases Raiders', *Evening Mail,* 27 September 1975.

[17] 'Woman Cashier Defied Fake Gun Raiders', *Evening Mail,* 24 August 1985.

[18] 'Manager Braved Gun to Capture Robber', 24 October 1985.

[19] 'Put Up Gun Screens, Building Society Told', *Birmingham Post,* 4 August 1982.

[20] 'Safety Screens Reversal', 4 January 1983.

[21] 'School Shop Window', *Evening Mail,* 2 December 1980; 'Pupils' Tasty Treat', *Evening Mail,* 27 November 1981.

[22] Derek Mee, 'Santa's Surprise for Birthday Girl', *Evening Mail,* 23 December 1983; and 'Artist in Society', *Evening Mail,* 11 November 1983.

[23] 'Cash Piles up to Help Blind', 'Winning Streak for Penny Pile Pub', *Sandwell Evening Mail,* 1 December 1983, *Sandwell Evening Mail,* 23 August 1983.

[24] 'Big Campaign to Teach Children Road Language', *Evening Mail,* 18 October 1984.

[25] Angela Paskin, 'Letter'.

End Notes: Chapter 6

[1] 'Mr West Bromwich closes his account', *Express and Star,* 12 May 2006.

[2] Annual Report and Accounts for the year ended 31st March, 1996.

End Notes: Chapter 7

[1] 'West Brom Appoint New Chief Executive', *Express and Star,* 11 May 2006.

[2] 'Stephen's Pledge', *Express and Star,* 13 May, 2006.

All other figures and quotes are taken either from *People*, the magazine of the West Bromwich Building Society, or from the Annual Reports and Accounts of the West Bromwich Building Society. I would like to thank Jim King, Communications Manager, for his invaluable help and advice in the writing of this chapter, and I also thank the Society's Denise McKenzie for her assistance.

End Notes: Chapter 8

I am indebted to Jim King, Communications Manager, for his involvement in the research and writing of this chapter.